It is impossible to live without failing at something, unless you live so cautiously that you might as well not have lived at all, in which case you have failed by default.

—J. K. ROWLING

FRACTURED BUT FEARLESS

S. IRFAN ALI, MD

FRACTURED BUT FEARLESS

Embracing the Art of Failing Forward

Forbes | Books

Published by Forbes Books, Charleston, South Carolina.
An imprint of Advantage Media Group.

Printed in the United States of America.

10 9 8 7 6 5 4 3 2 1

ISBN: 979-8-88750-593-0 (Hardcover)
ISBN: 979-8-88750-594-7 (eBook)

Library of Congress Control Number: 2025901510

Cover design by Matthew Morse.
Layout design by Ruthie Wood.

03-28-2025 4:46

For Ayra, Inshara, Ifah, Lucas, and Sofia—may each of you find your own path to happiness. Just know you are always loved.

To my parents, who instilled in us the values that guide our lives, and to my siblings, Naushaba, Faraz, and Asfia, whose love has always been unwavering.

To my friends, who are like brothers to me—thank you for your constant companionship.

To all the mentors who recognized my potential, especially Bruce Bergherm, Brook Longmaid, Brian Adams, Dr. Masood Khan, and my colleagues.

And to my wife, Ana—my rock, my confidante, and my greatest supporter—thank you for letting me be myself and for standing beside me every step of the way.

Since writing this book, my father has passed away. Someone once told me that losing a father is like having the roof torn away—I feel that deeply. Yet, he built a strong foundation for us to stand on, ensuring we would never be without shelter. Abba will be profoundly missed.

CONTENTS

NOTE TO THE READER

The paintings and photographs that accompany the beginning of each chapter are my original work, including the painting on the book cover. The pursuit of art is integral to my sense of self and serves as a source of resilience.

LEAP

As I was walking in a mall, I noticed this striking sculpture that captures the essence of a leap of faith. Suspended in mid-dive, arms outstretched, the human form symbolizes both vulnerability and strength, as if embracing the unknown with purpose.

It evokes a sense of controlled surrender—falling, yet still powerful, embodying the tension between risk and resolve. This reflects the idea of moving forward with purpose, even when the destination is uncertain.

INTRODUCTION
Embracing the Art of Failing Forward

I never lose; either I win or I learn.
—NELSON MANDELA

This book is not a memoir, nor am I its main character; however, my story does play a key role in it, for I cannot escape my own life, and the life I have lived has, of course, shaped my experiences. The same is true for you. Maybe you will see parts of yourself in these pages. I see this book more as lessons for living that have floated into my life like butterflies depositing drops of nectar on a weed struggling to push through a crack in the sidewalk. Long before I could see this book as having insights, it started with simple personal observations made as a doctor, an entrepreneur, a photographer, an artist, an immigrant; as a son, a father, a husband, a friend; and as a dreamer.

Decades ago, I used to write a blog, and one day a friend questioned me: "How do you know if anyone would care to read it?"

After some pondering, I replied, "My musings are like messages in a bottle. Imagine tossing a message in a bottle into the ocean. I would have minimal expectations that the bottle would survive the perils of the sea or that someone on the other side of the planet would find this message. Yet, if I do not cast the bottle into the ocean, it can never reach *any* destination."

Many have told me that my life has been so full of improbable events that it feels like something out of a story. As I have grown older, I have learned to see the valuable lessons that have arisen from my experiences, the people I have met, and the things I have observed. I don't think I am special in any way, but I do hope that even if only a handful of people discover this book, my attempt to cast messages out into the world won't be in vain, for one of the things my life has taught me is this: If you decide never to speak, there will be no dialogue.

This book is not a "how-to guide" of the modest success I have achieved. It might be more accurate to say it is a tribute to the lessons I learned through my experiences of failure. My life has been full of challenges. Whose isn't?

Mine has also been filled with opportunities—many missed; few captured. My experiences have carried me across continents. They have trained me professionally as a doctor, out of necessity as an entrepreneur, and out of desire as an artist. There have been a lot of highs and lows. Failures have abounded in all three ventures. But my diverse experiences have taught me that power is concealed within our falls, stumbles, and heartbreaks—even within our shattered dreams. Along the way, I have learned the hard way that brilliance rises from the ashes of defeat.

The nature of the world we live in is one where we celebrate champions, victors, and triumphant personalities to such a degree that we lose sight of how they arrived at their destination. We forget about the losses they suffered in order to get better, and we fail to acknowledge the resilience they have displayed in order to reach success. Similarly, too often we overlook the embedded wisdom acquired from our own failures.

I promised myself not to write an autobiography, and I'll hold to that promise, for ultimately this book is about "us," as in the collective "us" of humanity, but as you will see from the pieces of my life you will stumble across in these pages, I will share what I have come to observe about success and failure and about living in (and out of) balance. You will quickly see that many times I have lost sight of balance and have failed miserably. Yet you will also encounter an eternal optimist.

> If you decide never to speak, there will be no dialogue.

This is true despite a past that has included suffering sexual abuse as a child, being forced to watch my colleagues physically tortured, enduring lasting injuries by being beaten, performing hard labor despite having graduated medical school, navigating the bureaucracy of the US immigration system as a Pakistani man in the wake of 9/11, and telling patients they have terminal conditions or chronic diseases. Across these and other myriad events, hope sometimes was just a waning flicker of a dying flame.

But sometimes it was so bright that it extinguished despair and brought enduring power. My defeats hardened my resolve to believe that with time, even if I would fall, I would try to fall forward, ready to dust off and take another step. Hope continues to live in my heart because I am a firm believer that if you bring good to the world, the world will reciprocate, as long as you have the right intentions. Intentionality matters. Action matters more. Most of us tilt toward the "good" spectrum, for we are all shades of gray, harboring good and bad within ourselves. I believe that if we try to act upon the good parts of ourselves as much as we are able, then most likely good things will happen to us.

Another profound and insightful perspective I have learned the hard way is how often we are made to feel invisible. We need to become better informed on our deep understanding of the interconnectedness of humanity and the importance of recognizing every individual and their value, regardless of their perceived status. Perhaps we can look beyond the invisibility cloak and acknowledge the "invisible people" among us, recognizing those who pass unseen in our interconnected world.

Some of the stories and observations I share as I explore how we can overcome our setbacks are rooted in my humble upbringing in Karachi, Pakistan. I will share others from the daily human mysteries I encounter as a physician. I will draw additional insights from my juggling act of being the CEO of several healthcare organizations and the founder of the nonprofit Pioneer Medical Foundation while also trying to be a better son, brother, husband, father, and friend.

It is my hope that if you find value in the observations I share in these pages, you will come away with practical applications that can serve you in equal measure in the organizations of which you are a part, in your professional life, and, most importantly, in your personal life.

On this last point, a great deal has been written on work-life balance, but my essential stance is a simple one: if we do not find our personal lives full, engaging, creative, healthy, and rewarding, we can never be good humans, nor can we build genuine connections or become effective leaders or impactful participants in an organization that shares those traits. How we can make certain our lives are full and balanced and why this is so important underlies much of the structure of the ideas behind each chapter of this book.

You will also discover in me someone who can be a bit silly or eccentric as well as someone who loves finding joy in life. I like a good joke, and I'm guilty of making some bad ones. I like big ideas, but at the same time I try to keep things simple. I'm not one for fancy titles or obfuscating language. I am quick to experiment, love discovering new things, and sometimes come at things from what might seem like odd angles. I find that solutions can come from unexpected places.

There have been times when I couldn't see the optimism I now speak of nor view my life as fulfilling or engaging—moments when I simply felt stuck. Perhaps you are feeling stuck in your own life or believe you have reached a point of stagnation on your professional and personal journey. Whether you choose to read the book from start to finish or dabble in its ideas in an order of your own making, it is my wish that these "messages in a bottle" come as welcome surprises that stimulate your mind and generate renewed optimism for becoming unstuck.

Creating Connection: What This Book Can Mean for You

We often talk about our family legacies, our professional credentials, our grandiose triumphs and achievements. On the contrary, we don't hear much about the stories of our failures. Simply because it hurts, not many can talk about their shortcomings and disappointments. Silence is a coping mechanism and a grasp at self-preservation. Failing hurts our egos. It can make us doubt ourselves and reminds us that we are not infallible. When failure hits hard, it's crucial to pick up the pieces and bounce back faster and stronger. Those who can teach us the most have learned to face failure with grace. I don't pretend to be able to teach you anything, but I will share a number of my own fiascos in these pages. I've done my best to learn from them. Those discoveries shape a great deal of my thinking.

In this book, we will explore some practical strategies to analyze our missteps, reflect on the takeaways, refocus our efforts, and rejuvenate our spirits. Remember, a failure is just a temporary setback in this grand journey of life. By demystifying the notion of perfection, we create an environment that encourages others to realize from our shortcomings. Through sharing our stories and offering support to those who stumble, we ignite a spark of resilience equally meaningful in medicine, business, and our personal lives.

Remember, it is through failure that greatness is born.

As a friend once said to me, "Whatever mistake one makes, someone else has already made it. History repeats itself. It would be nothing short of egocentric not to see what went wrong the first time." Remember, it is through failure that greatness is born.

I invite you to join me as we embark on this journey of self-discovery and transformation, armed with the resilience to overcome any obstacle that stands in our way!

IMPERVIOUS

Sacsayhuamán, an ancient Inca fortress near Cusco, Peru. Massive, precisely cut stones are stacked together, forming walls that have withstood centuries of natural forces, from earthquakes to erosion. The stones are fitted so perfectly that not even a blade of grass can pass between them, showcasing the advanced engineering skills of the Inca civilization.

Though weathered and bearing cracks and fissures from centuries of exposure, the stones remain firmly interlocked, collectively holding up the structure. This fortress has endured despite these visible fractures, standing strong as a testament to resilience in the face of adversity.

People, too, may bear the marks of challenges, loss, and hardship in unity and resilience.

CHAPTER 1

Fractured but Fearless: Hard Knocks Teach Us Resilience

The human mind is a fearful instrument of adaptation, and in nothing is this more clearly shown than in its mysterious powers of resilience, self-protection, and self-healing.

—THOMAS WOLFE

Failure, as it turns out, is the antagonist neither to happiness nor to growth; rather, it is their reluctant mentor. Each stumble and setback I have experienced has been a harbinger of transformation, a whispered guide urging me to pay heed, to recalibrate, and to emerge wiser from the crucible of my own misjudgments. A life well lived is a dance of successes and failures. The failures inked on these pages are not inscriptions of inadequacy but rather brushstrokes painting a canvas of growth. Each oversight, each flawed decision, is a testament to a journey unafraid of imperfection, for it is not the absence of failure that defines us but our response to it—a response that echoes with the resilience to rise, the humility to learn, and the courage to turn the page, ready to script the next chapter with renewed vigor and seasoned wisdom. I've learned the lessons here, particularly the ones about my personal and professional growth, in a series of missteps, accidents, and stubborn, slow acceptance. I can't offer a guide so much as a map of my own experience, imperfect and always evolving.

Homeland

The city that shaped the beginning of these experiences, the city where I was raised—Karachi, Pakistan—is not conventionally known as an easy place to live. Sadly, it is a city often highlighted for its poor air quality, insane traffic, high crime rates, poor access to healthcare, and omnipresent heat. A massive city of over sixteen million people, it draws migrants from all over Pakistan and from many of its neighboring countries, and while work is readily available, it is a highly stratified place without much movement between classes. Its citizens have endured many periods of governmental corruption. It is a place that, for rich and poor, often requires profound endurance.

Like a lot of places around the world, while many of these challenges are true for the city at large, it is also a place filled with rich culture, lively people, and a joyous embrace of life. Art, literature, and music are vibrant and abundant. There is much I love about the city, and because many of the people I love live there, my vision of the place is a mix of personal affections and common observations. Duality about home places is common. Karachi was my home for the first twenty-seven years of my life, so it is simultaneously a city where I have fond memories of the festive atmosphere shared by family and

> Failure, as it turns out, is the antagonist neither to happiness nor to growth; rather, it is their reluctant mentor.

friends and, in contrast, I am also fully cognizant of its daily challenges, including conservative interpretations of Islamic law and the treatment of women.

My father, a physician, *chose* to serve in the slums, while my activist mother engaged in various causes, from creating schools to assisting incarcerated women. They both instilled a philosophy in me and my three siblings about being the kind of people who wish to make a difference in others' lives. They believed in doing good in whatever ways they could and raised us to share that belief. Despite my parents always being generous to others, our lifestyle was humble, although growing up, I never once felt that we had limited resources. No matter that we lived in a small home above my father's clinic. We felt like we lived in a mansion; we felt rich inside.

My father, now retired, had ample opportunities to serve affluent communities but chose to dedicate the early part of his professional life to those with scarce resources. Later, as a family practitioner, he would visit some of his patients at home a few times a day. I would tag along with him in the clinic and on house calls, and I always looked up to him and the way he carried himself, always graceful. He is old and frail now and has dementia. He may be smaller than he once was, but in my eyes he will always be a giant.

Always an introvert, he found his perfect balance when he and my mother, a consummate extrovert, were married. My mother is a serial activist, always working tirelessly in support of a good cause, be that creating schools for poor kids or establishing food pantries. She remains giving of her time and expertise even now, in her eighties.

One cause in which she has been involved throughout her adult life is working for nongovernmental organizations to provide legal assistance to women who have been unjustly incarcerated, something that is common in my part of the world, where women possess limited rights, have poor access to education and legal representation, and face high levels of domestic violence. In addition to her activism, my mother is also one of the most creative people I know. She has published six books, she paints, and she is a great poet. I don't claim to be a great painter, writer, or artist, but I believe that much of my creativity comes from her.

Despite unwavering support from my parents and their omnipresence as hardworking role models, for much of my early school life, I was always one of the worst students in the class. Certainly, this was true at least until the eighth grade, when I began to grow more serious about my studies. So, it remained a shock to many when, by a close margin, I was granted entrance to medical school. In an ironic application of stratification that is common throughout Asia, at least in my experience, parents who have had the opportunity to receive higher education in turn expect that their children will follow suit; choices were pretty binary. In a manner that can often serve as a punch line among comedians of Asian descent, those expectations get narrowed to "You can become a doctor or an engineer. Those are your choices."

My parents fell into this stereotype. I felt duty bound to become a doctor. I was certain I could not measure up, which left me terrified of disappointing my parents. I'd always been the *chota doctor* ("little doctor") following my father on his calls. In a rare moment when I voiced my lack of confidence about succeeding in becoming a doctor, my father sarcastically told me, "Don't worry. If you don't make it through medical school, I'll set you up with a tire stall. You can fix people's flats. There will always be a need for that."

I later learned that he had said something similar to my brother (who became an engineer!), promising to set him up as a rickshaw driver. Decades later, my brother joked with me: "You see, *Abba*

("Dad") is a thinker. I would have always had a place to take my rickshaw whenever I got a flat tire!"

I'd thought it took determination to live up to my parents' expectations and be accepted to medical school. I had no idea what tests of my resolve awaited me there. Apart from all the academic pressures, I also as a first-year medical student initially joined and later ran a student-body charity organization. Our objective was to provide free medications to those who often couldn't even afford food, let alone expensive antibiotics. Our team expanded our services to judiciously screen every unit of transfused blood for viral disorders, as drug abusers would often come to the blood bank and sell their blood. Those services were done under the auspices of a volunteer student organization called the Student Blood Transfusion Unit (SBTU).

Our services were free to the community but came at a cost to us on a personal level, for in Pakistan it is common for corrupt political groups to infiltrate universities, including the medical colleges, and many of those organizations are so fervent in their beliefs that they use violent tactics to try to indoctrinate students. In the process, some become little more than criminal organizations regularly using intimidation tactics and setting up racketeering schemes. They are exceedingly dangerous and can reach around the globe, not just within Pakistan. I attended medical school in the 1990s, and much of the Pakistani legacy of the Soviet war in neighboring Afghanistan and the fallout from their withdrawal there in 1989 was that the country was filled with violence spawned by the presence of drugs, guns, and aimless young men with no future or guidance.

As a student leader, I fell prey to one such organization that had its roots in advancing militant ethnic beliefs supported by its nasty criminal wing. My parents grew up in India and later migrated to Pakistan like most Muslims did, just as most Hindus moved to India in 1947 after the dissolution of the British Raj. Therefore, I was identified as being an Indian *Muhajir*, or "immigrant." Because I had been quite successful in fundraising from generous donors in support of the SBTU work, they identified me as a *Muhajir.* I was targeted by this group. I desired being no part of this organization.

The SBTU funds were also targeted because the criminal organization saw a way to make an easy buck. They approached me and demanded that I give them a portion of the donated funds each month. I implored them that it was not my money to give. But each time they returned with renewed demands, they raised the stakes and found new ways to terrorize us.

By the time I reached my final year of medical school, they had repeatedly tortured my colleagues and me, leaving us with emotional and physical scars, injuries that plague me to this day. On multiple occasions I was physically forced to witness them beating my colleagues, and I literally fled incidents where I witnessed them shooting several students and other bystanders from the medical college. Among many other witnessed criminal acts, I have a vivid memory of an event that occurred more than thirty years ago, when I found myself caught in crossfire between this gang and the police. I was literally running for my life while the bullets were flying by. Some of these memories are still fresh in my mind. As I look back, these events now seem shocking, but at the time we simply accepted them as part of life—just another day to endure and survive until the next.

One time I saw one of these terrorists creeping up behind a young kid who was minding his own business, and seconds later, this guy bludgeoned the kid's head with a thick plank of wood (the same plank of wood we sometimes used as a wicket while playing cricket). The kid fell face down like a toppled statue. Despite living among frequent violence, I felt so confused, unable to comprehend what

I had witnessed. Yet in so many ways, this was our way of living in those times.

Still, we soldiered on, confident in our cause. Among the other things we accomplished through SBTU, our best achievement was the acquisition of a storage space for medical supplies and cold storage for medications, including antibiotics. We poured our hearts and souls into this project. A few days after its completion, they raided our office and again tortured some of my senior colleagues. The next day when I arrived at the medical school, I saw smoke coming from our office. They had burned the storage facility, destroying all the medications and supplies we had stockpiled. Our years of work, our dreams, were literally incinerated in front of our eyes. My heart was crushed, and I sank to my knees.

Later that same day, during the sweltering afternoon heat, a young boy, probably around twelve or thirteen years old, walked into the smoldering area where our supplies were once stored. I learned that he had trekked several miles in the oppressive heat because someone had told him he could get free antibiotics here for his ailing mother, who had been admitted to a nearby hospital with pneumonia with severe sepsis. The antibiotic that could have saved her was among the other casualties of the arson.

I immediately began making phone calls and finally found a pharmacy that would provide me the antibiotic at a discount. I hopped on my little Honda 70 cc motorcycle and made the long trip to the pharmacy, which was in another part of the city. It took nearly ninety minutes round trip, but I was elated that I had the antibiotics in hand as I ran into Ward 5 of the hospital, where thirty or forty beds with sick patients were arranged in one large hall.

When I finally found the kid, he was standing at his mother's bed, holding her feet, sobbing. A sheet had been pulled over her head.

I had arrived a little too late to save her. This little boy was all alone. His mother could have been saved if not for the greed of others. In that moment, as sobs tore through the boy's fragile frame, a weight of defeat settled over me, heavy and unshakable.

I knew that I just needed to get through my last year of medical school, and then I had to depart from this place. If I stayed in Pakistan, and if those who wanted to harm me did not kill me, I would die of heartache at not being able to change the systems that had led to this woman's death.

But her death also lit a fire in me. I was determined to do my part in creating systemic changes that could prevent similar avoidable tragedies. I never let go of that boy or his mother, or of the feeling that I had failed them. But I could not accept that such failure had to be forever inevitable. It is impossible to look around a place like Karachi and neither see the kind of poverty that breaks my heart nor recognize how lucky I am to have been born to parents who had both the desire and the ability to create change.

A New Home Ground

Through more than two decades of working as a doctor in the United States, I have come to realize that, while not as pervasive, poverty exists here, too, as does desperation and hopelessness. As does resilience. In the US, as in Pakistan, I've also witnessed people refuse to give up, even though they seemingly have every reason to do so. Both heartache and triumph can move me to find strength within myself, something I feel acutely in the realization of the many ways my life has been blessed.

The applications of such lessons were immediately apparent from the day I arrived in the US—lessons made concrete because I was, at least in the financial sense, a poor man myself, landing in Chicago with $1,700 to my name. I came to Chicago because my ex-wife was there training as a medical resident in one of the hospitals, and through her I found a lead for a research position in Chicago and eventually secured that position as an associate researcher conducting leukemia research with Dr. Azra Raza, who took a chance on me and gave me my first job in healthcare in the United States. I was—I remain—grateful for this position.

I had graduated from medical school and, with help, escaped those who had tortured me, but I had completed only Step 1 of the United States Medical Licensing Exam (USMLE) and still needed to complete Step 2, without which I could not apply for a medical residency program.

Understandably, the pay during the research job was insufficient to meet my expenses, so I worked numerous odd jobs at night in order to stay afloat; my longest tenure at a job was cleaning carpets in office buildings. As a result, during some extremely hard, exhausting years in Chicago, each day I traded my white lab coat as a research scientist for blue coveralls, spending my nights working as a commercial carpet cleaner, mover, or delivery person.

Working radically different jobs offered a bit of whiplash, but no more so than trying to transition between two very different cultures. I'd watched my portion of American television, but nothing really prepared me for living there. Chicago winters could be as mean as Karachi summers. I remember one arctic-like night during my first winter in Chicago when I and a coworker were driving home after completing a job at Home Depot. I mean subzero. We were inside a running car, wearing down coats and still freezing, when we encountered a man huddled under a highway overpass. The city had issued shelter warnings for all residents. I knew that if this man remained outdoors, he would die.

I told my friend that we had to stop and check on him. This man was willing to go to a shelter but had been turned away every place he had tried, all saying that they were beyond capacity. I got him into the car and began making phone calls. Every facility I called was full. Exasperated, I knew what I had to do. I was staying with a friend that night, and we decided to provide shelter for him, at least for that night. We brought him to my friend's place, where he took a shower and ate whatever we had.

Watching him eat, I couldn't help but think that this was just one night for me—but this was his daily reality. Many times later in life, when dealing with some impatient clinicians who were frustrated with patients, I returned to that experience, saying to them, "Keep your composure and be kind to our patients, even when they are not. It is their *one* day with us, though for us it is just another day."

My actions offered no meaningful solution, no transformation that would keep him safe and warm beyond those few hours, but he certainly reminded me that someone *always* has it worse than us. I discovered that this man, a veteran, had been deprived of opportunities. After serving his country, he struggled to adapt to a "normal life." His challenges soon escalated as he turned to drugs to cope, which only compounded his difficulties. This acts as a reminder that the people we often overlook have their own stories and a full life, just like us. It's crucial to recognize our similarities and understand that none of us are too far from potentially facing similar circumstances.

Meanwhile, I was evaluating my prospects, including the chance, if I applied myself fully, to continue my education in a country those wishing to study medicine flock to from all over the world. With continued preparation for the USMLE and constant scrimping and saving over endless days that made me feel like I had a split personality—both halves of which seldom got sufficient sleep—I took and passed the exam. With a good deal of help from others—something that nearly always goes hand in hand with the realities of what it means to be resilient—I was able to secure a position in the radiology department at Beth Israel Deaconess Medical Center in Boston, the teaching hospital for Harvard. From there, I entered medical residency in the internal medicine program at the University of Massachusetts.

Residency is a fabled time of trials familiar to most people, even outside medicine. You eat, breathe—and almost never sleep—medicine. You are thrown into one impossible situation after the next, constantly aware that all the knowledge you thought you had gained in medical school is thrown into question when facing streams of new patients daily. Can you know enough? Can you remember what is required of you in a critical moment when a life is on the line? Can you truly serve patients when you must deliver awful, life-altering news, balancing the delicate task of offering hope in the face of despair—or on days when there is no hope at all, only the weight of bad news—and can you rise to the challenge of doing this with compassion and strength?

All the while, you are reminded of where you are in the pecking order and the knowledge that mistakes can cost lives. And typically you do it all while eating like crap while on the run. In my case, it also meant five years of living far away from my then-wife, who was halfway across the country continuing to advance her own training, and from my parents and siblings on the other side of the planet, all while in a place that could still feel baffling.

Some days then, when I had a moment to breathe, I marveled at the opportunities this country provides. Sometimes life's miracles come in small packages, and for me even something like the abundance of food available remained a wonder. There were things Americans took entirely for granted, things like aisles filled with food and canned goods of every variety. Abundant and cheap!

Sometimes, thinking about the uniform I used to wear doing other jobs, I am reminded that the white coat we wear as doctors is just another uniform. But how dare we call it a uniform? It's a white coat, not a cloak of wisdom, power, or perfection as some perceive. Yet the white coat does stand for something and comes with responsibility. We should feel honored to wear one.

When people hear the word *doctor*, they think *rich*. Well, you don't make crap while you're in your residency. The second day in this country and right off the boat, I asked my friend to take me to the cheapest grocery store. My total living food budget was about $125 a month, so canned goods looked like manna from heaven. I discovered quickly that with affordable items like canned tuna, vegetables of every kind, some rice, and the right spices, I could make a delicious curry. My culinary skills were equivalent to those of a toddler, and the end product often looked like an abomination, but it would do.

Walking down aisles and aisles of food, supplies, and household goods was overwhelming, and my budget was, unfortunately, underwhelming. I could get three cans of diced tomatoes for two dollars; garbanzo beans were even cheaper, and the price of canned tuna was for the birds. I grabbed the groceries and lived happily ever after for the next three weeks, cooking in the evening and getting my tips from a cookbook my mother had given me before I left. Before my arrival, I was lucky if I could make a cup of tea or fry an egg; I was awfully proud of myself and feeling pretty creative.

One day a friend accompanied me to my apartment.

He looked into my nearly empty refrigerator and asked, "What in the hell do you eat?"

The nosy sort, he moved on to my cabinets, where he exclaimed, "Do you have a cat?"

I had no idea what he was asking. "When would I have time to afford a cat?"

"Then why do you have all this cat food?"

"What in the hell are you talking about?" I asked.

He held up a can of "tuna" and pointed out with a sharp tongue, "Can't you see this picture of a cat in the background on all of your *tuna* cans?"

"Well, what about this giant picture of tuna in front," I said defensively. I didn't like his tone—it carried an unspoken assumption that he was smarter than me.

I continued with my defense. "I am struggling with your logic. I saw a cereal box at the market with a tiger on it. You guys don't have tigers in your house, do you? And as far as I know, tigers don't eat cereal. I will stick with what my mother said to me before I left. She said, 'If you put enough tomatoes in anything, it tastes good.'"

Well, I lost that battle and threw the rest of those cans away. Well, almost. I kept one just in case of a zombie apocalypse. Turns out you can make a mean curry out of cat food. Hit me up if you want my curry recipe. I apologize to all the dog people; I have nothing to offer!

Maybe minus the cat-food curry, life can be an awful lot like medical residency; you climb one seemingly unscalable mountain—like passing entrance exams for medical school—only to find the next mountain far steeper and taller, all while questioning if you have the proper climbing gear. Nobody really gives us a good map of the route that will get us to the top of the mountain, so we've got to try some things, run into a lot of dead ends, and search for another way up.

Success?

At the end of my time at Beth Israel in Boston and UMass, I was, in fulfillment of my parents' expectations, at long last able to practice as a doctor. Resilience, mental toughness, fortitude—whatever you want to label it—the hard work and lack of sleep had paid off . . . right? It would all be rose-colored glasses and unicorn dreams from here on out.

Not exactly. That's the thing about resilience; it's an ongoing condition, not a one and done. That's true for a simple reason—successful people always search out the next challenge, the next opportunity, which inherently means there is always another chance you might fail. I knew I would be tried in new ways. And I knew I had *so* much still to learn.

That's the thing about resilience; it's an ongoing condition, not a one and done. That's true for a simple reason–successful people always search out the next challenge, the next opportunity, which inherently means there is always another chance you might fail.

I remember receiving some distressing news one day about my visa. Without it, I could not continue my training. Yet if I was not admitted to a program, I could not renew my visa. I was completely lost, unsure of what to do or where to turn. Feeling utterly hopeless, I approached Dr. Brook Longmaid, our radiology fellowship program director, and sat down in his office with my head hung low. I whispered that I needed help. I explained that without a position, I faced deportation. I will never forget his response.

His reply was profound: "It takes a lot of courage to ask for help, Irfan. You've asked, and I will help."

Those simple yet profound words have stayed with me, and I've echoed them whenever someone has come to me for assistance.

He made the call on a speakerphone in front of me, saying to the other program director, "I apologize. We always take your best. I wish to return the favor. I will send you my best."

And that was that. I received a contract the next morning. I remain deeply grateful to Dr. Longmaid.

During my time in residency, like all young physicians, I quickly found myself continuously on call, suffering through hours that were no better than the split life I had been leading in Chicago or the impossible days at UMass, waking up most days before the sun came up and showing up at work to start prerounding in order to begin seven o'clock rounds, with many days ending at seven in the evening and others being on continuous thirty-six hour shifts.

The next major challenge was to find a place and a position where I could transfer my employment visa and find a sponsor for an H-1B visa allowing me to work as a physician in the US. Once again, without it, I would have to return to Pakistan. That opportunity arrived in the form of a hospital in Florida. The people who conducted my interviews seemed kind and supportive of young doctors. In hindsight, I can see that they were likely a little too kind.

Naive and trusting by nature, I was mesmerized by them and by the prospect of landing secure visa status doing the work I loved and was trained to do. I still remember sitting in my future employer's house when he handed me the contract, and asking, "Is this how all contracts are done?" When he assured me that was the case, I felt no reason to doubt him and signed without reading any details. I was completely ignorant about how "business" was conducted. Sometimes, at least in my case, we enhance our need for resilience with our own naivete.

I found a job and sponsorship for my visa in Florida and started working as a hospitalist. A few months after moving to Florida, I found myself working even longer hours than I had in residency. Just when I thought everything was fine, my former employers dug up the fine print in my contract and used it as an excuse to stop paying me. For me, it came down to a harsh choice: stay put and wait for my immigration papers or face deportation. I chose to stay.

I went entirely unpaid for fourteen months. I was afraid to call anyone or consult an attorney because I was certain that if I lost this job, I would be deported. I decided to suck it up until I got my green card. Talk about a feeling of failure. Without a paycheck, we were living on home equity loans and doing locum tenens (temporary positions) filling in the gaps for a hospital in Punta Gorda every other weekend, almost ninety minutes away from my home in Tampa.

I remember one day driving home from a weekend working in Punta Gorda, having arrived on Friday at 5:00 p.m. and being continuously on call until Monday at 7:00 a.m., when my ex-wife called and asked if I would stop and pick up some items for our kids. Our account was already overdrawn. How could I tell her that I didn't have a hundred dollars to my name that day, that I could not provide the essentials to feed us and our two kids, that I couldn't even buy them milk?

It gutted me. I pulled into a rest area where I often stopped when fatigued to take a nap. Exhausted, I didn't nap. I cried. I felt such shame. I was ready to give up on everything and return to Pakistan. The emotion seemed as strong as the one I'd felt in Karachi knowing I had to flee elsewhere if I were to survive.

Despite feeling like a total failure and wanting to return to Pakistan with my tail between my legs, I'm stubborn sometimes to a fault (the most fundamental element of resilience). I was determined to learn from my mistakes. I refused to let my employer define me as a failure. I fulfilled my five-year contract and found a position at another hospital.

When I gave them my notice, they threatened to sue me. They sent a letter through a lawyer demanding $140,000. While I had received no regular paychecks after the first fourteen months, the pay was meager, and I had no financial reserves. Several people advised me to just pay and get out. But I knew that what they had done was wrong; moreover, it was part of a larger pattern for how they did business and the way they preyed upon vulnerable foreign physicians, so I decided to take a stand.

I said, "I would rather go back to Pakistan than do involuntary servitude here." I had gathered enough evidence that they dared not pursue any legal action to make me pay them without incriminating themselves. After a year or so, they wrapped up in Florida and moved out of state. You know what? All that time in misery made me determined never to be naive again.

Lessons Learned

I set about purposefully studying every aspect of business. I spent more than a year studying intensely in every available hour. Taking online courses, I started with contracts and just kept going from there, essentially putting myself through an MBA-style curriculum. Today I am grateful to those employers who treated me and others so poorly. Because of them, I became a better person. Without those challenges, I would have never gained knowledge and a deeper insight. I hold no grudge toward them. It helped me to create a unique company.

Armed with this new knowledge, I started to understand the systems that drive healthcare and hospitals—their operations, finances, clinical outcomes, and interdependability. I came to realize that while healing our patients is the critical objective of healthcare, one could not do so without understanding fundamentals of the healthcare economy and how hospitals work, including learning their operations, finances, logistics, primary strategic zones, and guiding missions. All such knowledge comes together in our ability to heal someone in despair. I began to unravel the complex organizational and logistical challenges faced by hospitals, some of which created heavily bureaucratic and inefficient systems.

I would say that there are four career-defining philosophies I learned in my career that led me to create several successful ventures:

1. Focus on others. Early on, I learned a crucial lesson about success in both personal and professional life: *It's not all about you.* To truly succeed, you must understand and consider the needs of others and then tailor your approach and proposals accordingly to deliver real value.
2. Play the long game. Another valuable lesson came from a dear friend of mine, David Rippey. He said, "Don't always go for a home run; it might be short lived. Plan for the long game."
3. Create genuine relationships, and don't waste your time with people who bring negative energy to your life.
4. Explore what you are good at, and strive to be best at whatever niche you fill.

From the outset of my medical career, I discovered my passion for enhancing the quality of healthcare, a pursuit deeply aligned with my personal values. Quality in medicine is not just about achieving a five-star hospital rating; it's fundamentally about people's lives. Poor outcomes in healthcare affect real individuals—not just abstract "populations"—and can lead to the heartbreaking loss of someone's mother, father, or child.

Driven by this understanding, I focused intensely on improving healthcare outcomes. I became dedicated to providing best practices for the treatment of critical conditions such as congestive heart failure, sepsis, and stroke, among others. This journey to elevate healthcare quality began decades ago and has continually been at the forefront of my professional endeavors.

My commitment is rooted in a firm belief that high-quality medical care should be the norm, not the exception. Each patient's life and well-being hinge on the precision and efficacy of our medical interventions. Thus, my ongoing mission has been to ensure that our treatments not only meet but exceed standards, significantly enhancing patient outcomes and, ultimately, saving lives. This pursuit of excellence in healthcare quality is not just a professional obligation—it's a personal crusade fueled by a deep-seated passion to make a tangible difference in the lives of those we serve.

I remember the CEO of a hospital once asked me, "Dr. Ali, why do you want to expand your services to another market?"

I was silent for a moment and then replied, "*Destiny* is a very big word for a small man like me, but I feel this is mine. I don't have to fix everything, but I would like to do my part."

Quality is not just a dashboard but someone's mother surviving sepsis or a father being able to walk after a stroke. The more I studied and the more I observed conditions in hospitals, the more an idea began to take shape in my mind, a way that I might be able to maximize the difference I could make for my patients. *What if I started a healthcare company of my own with a strong emphasis on quality, culture, and compassion?*

This idea also aligned with an additional dream of mine. Even back in the Chicago days cleaning carpets, I used to imagine that if I was ever in a position to create employment, I would try to create *just* employment—not just for people who chose to work with me but their families too, to create a company where we were not constrained by org charts, corporate lingo, and write-ups, where firing someone didn't come easy, where people felt safe and appreciated. I wanted to create a system where people might see the future they desired rather than one they settled for. I wished to make a difference in people's lives professionally and personally and maybe inspire them to do the same. By that time, I had worked for ten years, always putting my patients first. But more and more I felt hampered by incompetencies and red tape that shackled me from making a change.

I eventually reached a point where one day I asked for a meeting with CEOs of the three hospitals who were my employers. I was nervous, as it's not an easy task to bring three busy CEOs to one table, especially for "just another doctor." After some small talk I said, "I want you to fire me." At first they laughed, assuming I was kidding. I explained that I wanted to start my own healthcare company. Once they realized I was serious, I urged, "If I fail, I'll crawl back to you on my hands and knees, and you can hire me back."

One CEO was absolutely opposed to the idea, and he said, "You are asking us to do the opposite of what every other healthcare organization is doing. Employment brings an alignment."

The second CEO, Bruce Bergherm, interjected, "If a person on the street comes into this room and asks this, the answer would be a definite no, but we are talking about Dr. Ali, and I would agree to this arrangement."

Brian Adams was the third CEO, and he agreed with Bruce. Years later, Brian said, "The best thing I ever did was to fire Dr. Ali. Look how it has helped thousands of our patients."

I hold that comment as a medal of honor, and I am grateful to them both.

I partnered with a fellow doctor who became a lifetime friend and mentor. I met Masood Khan somewhere around 2005. We complemented each other on so many different levels. We shared the value of placing our patients first and always treating them with dignity. In 2013, I started my first healthcare company, Pioneer Medical Group, and later created several other healthcare organizations. Our organization is still based on three pillars: compassion, great culture, and a laser focus on quality.

We focus on bringing state-of-the-art, evidence-based medicine to hospitals and postacute facilities built on teamwork and a belief that compassion is at the center of quality. My duty is to our patients and to the people who work with us. Their care always comes first. That belief is certainly a core value of the Hippocratic oath, but I don't think it makes me or my fellow physicians unique, for I believe we have to extend such principles into how we run our businesses and how we lead our lives.

Trying to treat others with compassion and respect can sound easy in a book. So can learning resilience. Both are a lot messier in life. The immediate period that led up to forming the Pioneer Medical Group was the most difficult time of my life, worse in many ways than being beaten by thugs. While that period was professionally challenging in ways that left me doubting my ability to succeed, my larger doubts were more personal. Doubts about my ability to provide for my family as I suffered from imposter syndrome. Doubts about who I fundamentally was. Difficulties accepting the scale of change I had undergone in the last decade

> Trying to treat others with compassion and respect can sound easy in a book. So can learning resilience. Both are a lot messier in life.

or more and the adjustments required to exchange one place and one culture for another.

All this also took a personal toll on my marital life. We drifted apart over time, went through trials, but could not make the marriage work. Divorce felt like indisputable failure to me. What took me even longer to accept was that I had been so busy trying to be successful, so consumed by the demands of work, that I'd lost parts of myself along the way.

I had to reach a point in my life—both in age and experience—where I could create the space necessary for true introspection. Perhaps the greatest lesson I've embraced is this: To succeed, you must first know yourself intimately enough to define what success truly means to you. Along the way, I've learned two crucial lessons, which I'll explore in greater detail later in this book:

1. No one can make you happy; happiness must be found within.
2. Heal yourself first, for only the whole can truly mend the broken.

I had to learn to be comfortable in my own skin. I don't know how anyone can face hurdles and overcome them without that knowledge. Only then might we find the resilience to rise and the humility to learn.

Perhaps that is where we should begin. There will be a lot of failing down along the way to success and a lot of difficult lessons, most of which we will have to learn multiple times. But I can testify that it is so worth the effort, for despite hardships along the way, I have been blessed with a full heart and an amazing life.

SANCTUARY OF STILLNESS

This image speaks to the power of self-reflection—stepping away from the outside world to find clarity within. The woman's quiet presence in this sanctuary-like space reminds me of the importance of retreating inward to reconnect with ourselves, letting go of external pressures, and finding strength in silence.

In a world often dominated by noise and busyness, this sanctuary of stillness captures a rare, valuable pause—a reminder that peace and understanding lie not outside but within, patiently waiting to be found.

CHAPTER 2

Looking Back to Move Forward: Reflection and Renewal

And they call again, "It's simple," they say,

"and you too have come

into the world to do this, to go easy, to be filled

with light, and to shine."

—MARY OLIVER, "WHEN I AM AMONG THE TREES"

We all face hardship. It's impossible to be a human and not. Usually, the things that challenge us seem like impossible obstacles at the time. Of course, a lot of my barriers proved to be of my own making because I can be an idiot at times, proving naive. And other times I may have a unique perspective of what some see as an unconventional way of looking at things. But I can't change the way I think any more than I can change where I was born. It was not always easy.

In the beginning, fortitude didn't come naturally. I didn't always do well when faced with an obstacle. Sometimes, looking back, I am baffled at why I allowed myself to feel so overwhelmed. Other times, I do wonder how I got through it at all. And once in a while, those backward glances can seem downright comical.

Early in my life, whenever I felt like I was facing an insurmountable wall with nowhere to turn, I would engage in a mental exercise. I'd ask myself, *When was the last time I faced a similar situation when it seemed there was no light at the end of the tunnel?* Remarkably, each time, I realized that I had managed to find a way through. This practice is inspired by the words of Winston Churchill: "If you're going through hell, keep going." His wisdom has stayed with me. To this day, whenever I feel completely stumped, I reflect on past challenges, which helps me regain my composure and strategize a solution. This method of looking back to move forward has become a crucial tool in navigating the uncertainties of my life and career.

Hustling

As I have shared, during my time in Chicago, I worked numerous odd jobs to support my meager pay doing cancer research. (Again, I am not being ungrateful; I was lucky to at least have one stable job). It was a constant race, rushing from my day job as a research assistant to whatever gig I had lined up next. My first odd job was a brief but memorable stint at a Chinese restaurant. For the record, this is the only job from which I've ever been unceremoniously dismissed. My first day on the job started on a promising Saturday morning. I swept, mopped, and conquered a mountain of dishes.

While I labored, I could almost see my future unfolding, my pathway to saving for my future. But then the plot thickened with the introduction of vegetables. And not just any veggies—I was faced with a Mount Everest of tomatoes, carrots, and potatoes, all demanding to be peeled and chopped before my shift ended. With time ticking away, I pondered how to streamline this herculean task into an efficient operation. Determining how to break tasks into manageable processes is simply how my mind works.

As I stood there, lost in strategic thought, my boss appeared. "Why aren't you working?" he demanded. Proudly, I explained that my pause was all in the name of efficiency, planning the best approach to tackle the veggie monolith. His expression quickly morphed from curious to thunderous. "Man, these are just damn vegetables, not rocket science. *You are fired!*" he declared.

Shuffling out of the kitchen on my walk of shame, I couldn't resist asking for my day's pay. He begrudgingly handed over half. As I glanced down at the meager change in my hand, I shot back, "Hey, can I at least grab some hot and sour soup on my way out?" Sipping that soup later that night, I savored it more than any gourmet meal. You live, you learn, and sometimes you even get soup.

It's the learning part most of us struggle with. If we don't learn, then we're not practicing resilience; we're just stuck like a song on repeat. My Chinese restaurant dismissal set the stage for a series of hustles: delivering pizzas, assisting with moving services, and cleaning carpets. The grind was relentless. I vividly recall the reasons I was hired—and why I was sometimes rejected. At one pizza joint on Lakeshore Drive, the owner turned me away for being overqualified.

> If we don't learn, then we're not practicing resilience; we're just stuck like a song on repeat.

That rejection was nothing compared to an event that transpired at a job I landed with a moving company. Did I mention naivete? It was a bitterly cold winter in the Windy City, which truly lived up to its name, with slippery roads to boot. A friend and I had spent the whole day helping a family move from Schaumburg to Evanston. Just as we were finishing, a man who had been watching us approached. He said he lived nearby and needed help moving some items. He already had a truck but told us that he suffered from back pain, making it impossible for him to manage on his own. He offered us twenty dollars an hour. We normally earned just over seven dollars an hour, so I was overjoyed. I told my friend, "We could retire after this job."

We agreed to help him and met him outside his apartment an hour later. He let us know that not everything needed moving since he shared the place with a roommate. Just a few choice items: a TV, couch, computers, and some paintings. After three hours of heavy lifting transporting the items from the third floor, everything was neatly packed in his truck. He sat in the truck's cab. As soon as I closed the truck's loading door, he floored it. My friend and I sprinted after the fleeing truck, screaming at the top of our lungs, "Hey, pay up! You owe us money!" Unfazed, he kept driving. Then, popping his head out and showing us a cheeky grin, he hollered back, "Dude, that wasn't even my apartment!"

It took a moment to register, but then it hit me: We'd just helped this guy commit a robbery. My friend turned to me, blissfully ignorant of our new "criminal" status, and suggested, "Let's call the police."

I stared at him and said, "Think about it. How do you suppose it'll sound to the cops? 'Hi, we didn't get paid for helping our boss with a burglary.' We're just two fresh-off-the-boat immigrants; how do you think that will go?" That day, we decided to cut our losses. And no, I definitely couldn't retire.

Years later, every time I needed fingerprinting for a medical license or immigration paperwork, I'd panic. Whenever that fingerprint scanner flashed its red light, signaling a misalignment, my first thought was always to run before I ended up in jail. I even imagined having to explain to my dad, "Instead of pursuing a career in medicine, I got arrested for grabbing and dashing out with a leather sofa and a TV." Yeah, that would not have gone over well. As I look back, it's almost funny how those moments at the fingerprint scanner turned me into a nervous wreck.

For a long time, I chastised myself for being so gullible. I'd allowed myself to play out a scenario about immigrants on a bad sitcom. But sometimes the obstacles we face that will require the self-improvement needed to realize resilience aren't so comical, and much of the time they arrive when least expected and through forces we can't imagine.

Hard Reminders

After Chicago, I moved to Boston in 2000. I had passed my licensing exams and applied to numerous programs. I got a surprise call about a possible position in Boston, as someone had dropped out at the last minute. I interviewed for it and was accepted. I moved to Boston, where I fell in love with the city but hated the cold.

I loved working at Beth Israel Deaconess Medical Center. I remain utterly grateful to Dr. Sughra Raza, Dr. Janet Baum, and Dr. Brook Longmaid, my attending physicians. So much of what they taught me remains not just central to the work I do as a doctor; the ideals they represented about patient care and quality guides the work we do at the Pioneer Medical Group. At long last I was making good on the very reason I had come to America and firmly on my path to becoming a practicing physician.

Then 9/11 happened.

I had first seen the Twin Towers in 1991, when my father took me, my mother, and my sister to New York. I stood in awe looking at these majestic structures. Like people all over the world, I was shocked and dismayed when terrorists attacked the World Trade Center by hijacking commercial airliners, both flights originating from Boston where I lived. I couldn't believe that the news reports were true. The towers were gone, those iconic structures reduced to rubble, destroyed in a moment of senseless violence, transformed from symbols of commerce to gravestones for nearly three thousand innocent civilians.

The perpetrators, in some superficial ways, resembled me, including sharing the same religion, but their understanding of faith was so misguided that they altered the course of history. The 9/11 attack was a painful reminder of how the actions of a few can unjustly affect the perception of many. These zealots and so-called keepers of faith gave in to their twisted beliefs and listened to the personal demons that cajoled them to transform themselves into flying weapons of death and misery. They didn't just hijack the planes; they hijacked a faith.

The term *jihad* in Islam carries a rich and complex meaning, often misunderstood or misrepresented in broader public discourse. Primarily, *jihad* means "struggle" or "effort" in Arabic, and it refers to striving in the way of God. This concept is broad, encompassing internal, personal struggles against sin. The most significant battle any person can wage is against their own impulses in order to follow the righteous and moral path. The most important component in this inner battle relates to self-improvement, purification, and personal growth.

The crazy fanatics who misinterpreted *jihad* as "death to infidels" not only killed and maimed people they had never met; their misguided crimes resulted in hijacking Islam, robbing millions of people of their identity and their dignity. For Muslims, the aftermath of 9/11 marked a significant shift in how they were perceived and treated worldwide. This tragic event not only led to immediate fear and sorrow but also triggered widespread suspicion and scrutiny toward Muslim communities.

In the years following 9/11, Muslims found themselves having to navigate an increasingly hostile social and political landscape. Stereotypes and misconceptions about Islam and its followers proliferated, often fueled by media portrayals and political rhetoric, which did not always distinguish between extremists and peaceful Muslims, who represent the vast majority. This generalization led to a spike in Islamophobia, hate crimes, and discrimination, forcing many Muslims to defend their faith and assert their identities more vigorously than ever. One of the most painful questions frequently asked of me was "So, how do you feel about 9/11?"

What was I supposed to say? It would be like asking someone, "How do you feel about Nazis?"

The repercussions extended beyond personal prejudice to impact policy and governance. Initiatives like the USA PATRIOT Act and the Special Registration process sought to strengthen national security but also raised concerns about racial profiling and impinging on civil liberties. Many Muslims felt unfairly targeted by these measures, further complicating their efforts to integrate and participate in communities, especially in Western countries. Special Registration required certain noncitizen males over the age of sixteen from specific countries, including Pakistan, to register with the federal government.

The night before my required Special Registration interview, I found myself enveloped in a cloud of anxiety and fear. As I lay unable to sleep, the darkness amplified my worries about the upcoming interrogation. My mind raced with countless scenarios, each more daunting than the last. The thought of being scrutinized and judged on every word and gesture was suffocating.

That night I kept thinking of other such "special" measures in history. The Chinese Exclusion Act (1882) was the first significant law restricting immigration based on race and nationality. It prohibited all immigration of Chinese laborers and was initially intended to last for ten years but was eventually extended.[1] After the attack on Pearl Harbor in 1941, over 120,000 Japanese Americans were forcibly relocated and incarcerated in internment camps across the United States. This action was also "justified" by the government as a national security measure against potential espionage or sabotage.[2] Another was Operation Wetback (1954). This nationwide campaign was to remove illegal immigrants, primarily Mexicans. Like Special Registration, all these policies were based on group identity rather than individual guilt or suspicion.

Despite my worries about meeting with the immigration officer in downtown Boston, the interview experience turned out to be unexpectedly pleasant. The officer was not only respectful but seemed almost apologetic during our interaction. However, as I headed home after being registered as "special," I couldn't help but feel that the label didn't make me feel very special at all. The contrast between the courteous meeting and the heavy reality of the designation left me with mixed emotions, dominated by a pervasive anxiety to demonstrate to others that I was a "good Muslim."

This urge to clarify my identity was strong, even though, ironically, I've never been very devout. My relationship with organized

1 "Chinese Exclusion Act (1882)," National Archives, https://www.archives.gov/milestone-documents/chinese-exclusion-act#:~:text=This%20act%20provided%20an%20absolute,good%20order%20of%20certain%20localities.

2 "Japanese-American Incarceration During World War II," National Archives, https://www.archives.gov/education/lessons/japanese-relocation.

religion has always been complicated, marked by personal struggles and doubts. Perhaps the pressure was more internal, a self-imposed expectation to provide some sort of clarity about who I was in the midst of broad misunderstandings.

One time, while trying to catch a flight from Tampa to Whistler, Canada, for a skiing trip with my kids, the usual chaos ensued—I couldn't print my boarding pass at the kiosk and had to approach the counter. My two daughters, Inshara and Ayra, aged six and eight then, waited patiently as I explained the situation to the flight representative. As I requested my boarding pass, the gate agent looked at me quizzically and asked, "Is your boarding pass not printing because you are on the list?"

Her question echoed across the crowded lounge, drawing the attention of many other people. Suddenly, the woman standing behind me raised her voice and inquired, "Is he on the terrorist list?" An awkward silence fell over the line, now thick with tension.

After eventually receiving my boarding pass and boarding the flight, I couldn't shake the feeling of being targeted. Throughout the flight, I was so self-conscious that I refrained from even using the bathroom, noticing several passengers glancing at me as if I were a "person of interest." The whole experience made me feel like I was under some kind of suspicion, adding an unwelcome layer of stress to what should have been a joyful family getaway.

We All Fall Down

Naivete, cultural ignorance, vast social or political history—the point I want to make is that these narratives are examples of *my* struggles. Mine are different than yours. Yours are every bit as real and as meaningful (and can seem as insurmountable and occasionally comical).

We all—your sibling, your neighbor, your colleague—face different challenges, and the weight of those struggles can feel heavy. Despite the nature of these difficulties, it's crucial to maintain a clear head and strive to understand who you truly are. It helps me when I understand that all your troubles, stressors, and calamities are as equal, as important, and as real as mine, just a bit different.

Are you going to author your own story, or will you become a character in someone else's? What makes you fundamentally you? Not just the sum of your experiences but the core of who you are and what values you cherish. I have learned the hard way that I must live in the present. While we can shape our future, the past is unchangeable. Dwelling on it will only leave us stuck in the present, unable to move forward.

Success and failure, each setback becomes a thread that weaves a story of resilience. The key to becoming resilient lies not in avoiding failure but in using it as a stepping stone toward greater achievements. Those we admire for their ability to stick to their course exemplify that success is not a linear journey but a mosaic of meandering paths marked by trials and triumphs, with failure serving as a catalyst for personal and professional evolution. Some of those most celebrated for their achievements are not immune to the shadows of failure. History is replete with tales of accomplished individuals who, despite their triumphs, faced setbacks that tested their resilience. These stories serve as reminders that even the most triumphant journeys encounter stumbling blocks.

Success and failure, each setback becomes a thread that weaves a story of resilience.

Our experiences shape who we are, but it's ultimately up to us to decide how they define us. Just as the sun gives meaning to the night, allowing us to appreciate the cool serenity it brings, and the night in turn enhances our appreciation for the warmth and light of day, so too do our emotional experiences complement each other. Without grief, we wouldn't fully appreciate joy in our lives.

Our failures and tough experiences are like the waves in a vast sea that, in their ceaseless ebb and flow, offer a mesmerizing glimpse into the rhythms of our lives. Like us, they are driven by forces, in their case responding to the gravitational force of the moon and driven by the power of wind across the water's surface. Our lives are not so different, pulled by family, success, fame, money, and other forces. If we lack the strength and will to navigate them, we can get lost. However, if we equip ourselves with the right tools to face these challenges, they can help us grow into more complete, compassionate individuals. This balance and integration of experiences allow us to develop a fuller understanding of ourselves and the world around us, ultimately leading to a more harmonious and empathic life.

When faced with adversities, it is crucial to reflect on opportunities and consider what could have been done differently. It is a practice akin to falling forward—each time you stumble, it's an opportunity to learn and grow. While it may not always lead to immediate success, this approach is crucial for personal development. Each fall, each challenge is a lesson that prepares you for the next step.

The key is to rise each time you fall, dust yourself off, and continue moving forward with determination and your head held high. This resilience and relentless pursuit of growth, even in the face of setbacks, is what ultimately shapes character and leads to success.

Building resilience involves developing a set of tools and strategies that can help you navigate through tough times effectively. Here are some of mine:

Tools to Navigate Adversities

1. Mindfulness

Mindfulness practices and meditation are often recommended as primary tools for mental strength and resilience, yet traditional meditation doesn't work for everyone. Personally, I've found that sitting still and trying to quiet my mind is nearly impossible. Instead, my hobbies have become my meditation. Whether I'm meticulously working on a small piece of metal for hours, painting, or sculpting, these activities allow me to lose myself completely, focusing deeply without distraction. During these moments, nothing else matters, and I am fully immersed. This intense concentration and engagement in doing what I love acts as my form of mindfulness. It calms my mind, reduces stress, and helps regulate my emotions. I encourage everyone to find their own unique "meditation," whether it's a creative pursuit, a physical activity, prayers, or something entirely different.

Discovering what truly allows you to achieve a state of presence can be a powerful tool to enhance your ability to handle life's challenges. And as an extension of whatever mindfulness tool works for you, your body must carry its part, so remember that even some level of exercise or maintaining a healthy lifestyle can enhance your ability to handle stress.

2. Emotional Awareness

It has taken me a considerable amount of time to understand even the most fundamental aspects of my emotional vulnerabilities. In my experience, self-discovery is a critical first step toward achieving any goal. More importantly, it's essential for maintaining one's mental health and emotional stability. Over time, I've developed an internal gauge that helps me recognize when someone else is offloading their emotional turmoil onto me. This same gauge also guides my responses in unstable or challenging situations, allowing me to manage my reactions more effectively. Understanding these aspects of myself has been key to navigating both personal and professional interactions. This provides me with an ability to better deal with my own internal conflicts and enables a healthier approach to life's ups and downs.

3. The Power of Relationships

I firmly believe in the power of cultivating genuine, lasting, and deep connections. Building strong, supportive relationships with friends, family, and colleagues not only provides a buffer against the effects of stress but also makes it easier to manage crises. No matter our position, title, or level of success, life is unpredictable, and any aspect—be it financial stability, relationships, or social status—can falter. However, having a trusted circle of people who care about you can cushion the impact of such falls. The support from loved ones can make a significant difference during tough times, and it's essential to offer the same support in return.

4. Optimism

I hold a balanced view on optimism. While I don't subscribe to absolute optimism, which can sometimes feel unrealistic, I do embrace a form of cautious optimism. This approach means maintaining a hopeful outlook while being aware of the realities of any given situation. Surprisingly, this tempered optimism can often bring about positive outcomes, almost as if you're manifesting what you hope for. Applying cautious optimism toward people can also strengthen relationships.

Evidence suggests that when we hold higher expectations for children, they tend to rise to the occasion.[3] The same principle applies to adults. By believing in the potential and capabilities of those around us, we can encourage them to achieve more than they might in an environment of doubt or negativity. This balanced optimism not only fosters personal growth but also builds trust and boosts morale among peers, family, and friends. It's about seeing the glass as half full but being prepared in case it spills.

5. Nimbleness

Being flexible and adaptable in your thinking and approach allows you to respond more effectively to change and uncertainty. This adaptability can be crucial in dealing with complex situations that are beyond your control.

As a healthcare professional and an executive, I experienced firsthand the immense challenges brought on by the COVID-19 crisis. The pandemic turned the world upside down, placing extraordinary financial strains on our organizations and putting immense pressure on the morale of healthcare workers. It was a perfect storm that tested the resilience of everyone involved. This period also highlighted the importance of adaptability in crisis management.

As an organization, we survived these unprecedented challenges because we had cultivated a culture of agility. We trained ourselves to be nimble, to adapt quickly to changing circumstances, not to take advantage of the situation, and to find innovative solutions under pressure. This ability to swivel and adjust to the rapidly evolving

3 W. B. Brookover, review of "Pygmalion in the Classroom: Teacher Expectation and Pupils' Intellectual Development," by R. Rosenthal and L. Jacobson, *American Sociological Review* 34, no. 2 (1969): 283–283, https://doi.org/10.2307/2092211.

situation was crucial in navigating the pandemic effectively. The experience underscored the value of preparedness and flexibility in overcoming severe disruptions and continuing to provide essential services amid adversity.

Our ability to survive the adversity of COVID-19 is a prime example of how all five principles I have outlined coalesced. Time was in short supply and demands could seem impossibly heavy, but encouraging mindfulness when outside the hospital or clinics to recenter, find our true north, and reconnect with the people in our personal lives helped us take the next step required each day. Becoming in tune with ourselves also helped us be aware of how we communicated with our families, our teams, our patients, and our families, encouraging us to confront our emotions and demonstrate care and intentionality when we exchanged concerns, instructions, and observations and when we asked questions.

We maintained the mindset that we were all in this together working toward a shared goal, acknowledged the difficulties we faced but embraced cautious optimism that we would get through it if we could prove nimble enough to adapt to ever-changing circumstances. The result of demonstrating tenacity in a crisis has allowed us to thrive in the years that followed.

These five strategies can help us become like a tree in the wind, our roots spread so wide and with such a tight hold on the earth that we can be bent violently and not break. We've all seen cable news footage taken by camera operators sent out into the violence of a hurricane of trees thrashing in the wind, some bent so that their crowns nearly touch the ground, and yet once the storm passes, there they are, upright once again, perhaps missing a limb or stripped of their leaves but alive and resilient. What's more, they can heal at the broken places, and they will return to full leaf the next season.

But it is important to acknowledge that before we can be resilient, I cannot underscore sufficiently the underlying power of kindness and compassion—which necessarily includes kindness and compassion first toward *yourself*. Our struggles with self-compassion often mirror the difficulty of nurturing a plant struggling to survive in barren soil. Just as harsh conditions can inhibit growth, a harsh self-judgment can prevent the nurturing of our spirit. The roots of this self-criticism lie in our fear of failing again, embarrassment, and a fear of falling due to cultural complacency—many worry that accepting their flaws might stop them from striving for improvement.

I am certain that self-compassion is not equivalent to surrender; it's emotional resilience. It is not a tool to soften the blow but one that allows us to review our steps through different lenses. Sometimes you need a wide-angle lens and sometimes a macro lens. Self-compassion transforms our inner narrative from one of isolation and inadequacy to one of learning and shared human experience. Just as gentle rains revive the earth, our kind words can soothe our bruised psyches and foster an environment where we can learn from our mistakes rather than be defined by them.

Before you can be good to someone else, you have to feel good about yourself. None of us are perfect. I think I've established by now that I'm certainly not—hello vegetable mountain and accidental robbery. We all have to learn to forgive ourselves, an allowance that is not to be confused with having no remorse, for without remorse there is no moving forward. It's essential to understand that remorse isn't just about regret—it's a stepping stone toward betterment.

As we prepare to explore further, I always think about a saying I've heard before, one for which I don't know the source, so I can only paraphrase: "Forgiving yourself, believing in yourself, and choosing to love yourself are the best gifts one can receive."

TEARLESS

I created this painting depicting a woman in sorrow, her expression somber and introspective. Her body language—head resting on her hand, shoulders slouched, eyes gazing downward—conveys a heavy emotional weight. The background is fragmented and abstract, with angular shapes and intersecting lines, mirroring the woman's fractured emotional state. The use of blue, typically associated with sadness and introspection, reinforces her mood, while the absence of warm colors leaves the painting feeling distant, as though she is enclosed in her own world of pain.

CHAPTER 3

Tears in the Rain: Searching for Peace of Mind

"Did you really want to die?"

"No one commits suicide because they want to die."

"Then why do they do it?"

"Because they want to stop the pain."

–TIFFANIE DEBARTOLO, *HOW TO KILL A ROCK STAR*

One of the significant hurdles I faced, particularly in my early years, was navigating a downward spiral triggered by stressors, setbacks, and disappointments. I found myself responding to these challenges with anger, self-isolation, or escapism. I desperately needed something, someone, or some defeat of an ancient, powerful part of my brain to become unstuck.

I had entered medicine to do my part to make the world a little bit of a better place, yet too often I became consumed not by what I was doing right but by my faults and failures. Sometimes we all are zipping away in life, and we miss the good stuff. As I share a story of my experience with a patient who profoundly impacted my life, I encourage you to pause your reading and reflect on your own poignant experiences. Consider what alternative actions you might have taken when you reflect on a crossroad moment of your own life. I believe that such introspection is instrumental in redirecting our focus and revitalizing our perspective. While it may not always provide a cure, reflection can be a valuable aid in the process.

A crossroad moment in my life occurred during a patient encounter that happened decades ago. It led me to question the true impact I was having on peoples' lives. It happened on a night when, despite living in Florida, the air was unusually chilly. The cold night air matched my heavy mood. The day had been long, and exhaustion weighed heavily on me. It was well past ten o'clock when I climbed into my car and began the journey home from the hospital. Having spent the majority of my day tending to patients, a good deal of it in the intensive care unit, I was physically and emotionally drained.

Shortly before leaving the hospital, I had engaged in a profound and emotionally taxing conversation with a patient and his family. I hope it never becomes just routine to impart bad news to anyone, especially my patients. The discussion involved delivering the devastating news to a seemingly healthy forty-nine-year-old man, in front of his two daughters, that scans had revealed he had terminal lung cancer with metastasis to the spine. The gravity of that conversation lingered in me, casting a cold shadow. As I walked out of the room, I couldn't stop thinking that I also had two daughters at that time, and it was impossible to deny the parallel thoughts in my mind.

As I set out for home, despite the weariness that clung to me from the day, anticipation warmed my spirit at the thought of seeing my daughters and planting a kiss on their cheeks. However, that anticipation was disrupted by an abrupt text from the hospital to call back urgently. I did what doctors swear a sacred oath to do—I called back.

"Doc, there's a new consultation," a nurse conveyed, her voice tinged with urgency. "You've got a thirty-three-year-old woman brought in after a suicide attempt. The psychiatrist is requesting an immediate medical clearance."

I asked for more details. The nurse elucidated, "She slit both her wrists and was discovered by her sister, who brought her to the emergency department."

I murmured, "I'll make my way there shortly." So much for going home to my family. Another family was in crisis. I made a U-turn.

At the hospital. I swiped my ID card and entered the secured psychiatric floor keenly aware of that distinctive hospital scent. Every time I enter this secured wing, I feel guilty knowing that I can get in and out anytime I want, and its occupants can't. It was after eleven, and as I walked through the brightly lit corridor, I thought, *These lights will strip me of my sanity at night.*

The guard noticed my white coat and allowed me to enter the behavioral floor. Our white coats work as cloaks. Sometimes others, even doctors, forget that it is just another uniform, a very privileged uniform. Those donning white coats do carry a heavier burden and an even heavier responsibility—for they are symbols of trust, wisdom, and hope. People often overlook the struggles, demons, and personal battles that individuals might be facing behind the facade of presumed stability. Under the coats we all have the same insecurities, sensitivities, and weakness, no matter our training and knowledge.

Heading directly to the nursing station, I found the nurse who had paged me seated there. After exchanging greetings, I asked, "Hey, can you come with me to see this patient?" I like to have a second set of eyes and ears when meeting patients, other perspectives that might recognize something I miss. Nurses are invaluable members of the hospital team and tend to have deeper connections with patients. A nurse can help create an atmosphere of security and comfort. Not this time. Instead of accompanying me, the nurse simply gestured toward the patient's room. Not the most promising start.

From the corridor, I could hear muffled cries emanating from within the room. Stepping in, as always, my persona shifted. I left my life outside the room and immersed myself in practicing the art of medicine, which to me means acknowledging its inherent uncertainty and surprises, recognizing it as more art than an exact science.

The room exuded a dim ambiance, exacerbated by the dark gray curtains on the windows. Two beds occupied each side of the room, and on the bed on the left, she sat, clad in a hospital gown, huddled with her body enveloped in a hospital blanket. Cradling her knees, she swayed gently back and forth, emitting occasional muffled cries, as if trying to minimize any disturbance.

Both her wrists were like a fractured branch hastily bound with bandages, masking the deep wounds beneath. The bandages, a thin layer of false calm, barely concealed the raw, aching pain that coursed through her—an imperfect shield against the darkness she had tried to escape, while the rest of her still stood, fragile but longing to mend. Her pallid complexion hinted at anemia, or perhaps her skin tone was merely a product of the subdued lighting. She appeared unaware of my presence.

Her disheveled hair, wrinkled skin, and hollow eyes told a silent tale of her distress. Although she was only thirty-three years old, I could see that life had taken a toll on her. Once she looked up and made eye contact, she tried to appear strong, but the occasional tears that dropped from her eyes and escaping sobs were not helping her efforts. This marked her third admission following suicidal attempts, leaving no doubt that she was in desperate need of help.

Sitting down beside her, I was aware that my immediate responsibility was to ensure her medical clearance for impending psychiatric treatment. Examining her chart, I saw that all the checkboxes were ticked: labs were almost fine, no significant anemia, X-rays were normal—she appeared medically stable. However, the emotional turmoil she harbored within told a different story. I put aside her chart and initiated a conversation.

> The bandages, a thin layer of false calm, barely concealed the raw, aching pain that coursed through her—an imperfect shield against the darkness she had tried to escape.

As our conversation unfolded, she gradually began to share the harrowing chapters of her life. She started to calm down and willingly shared details. Her history revealed a painful narrative of enduring abuse at various stages: As a child, she was sexually victimized by her father; while a teenager, she was subjected to the trauma of assault by classmates; and presently, as a wife, she grappled with abuse from her ex- and current husband. Like many others in abusive relationships, she had been in a vicious cycle of violence.

The physical toll of her tumultuous experiences manifested in a conspicuous scar on her abdomen. This visible mark bore witness to a particularly brutal incident when her ex-husband's forceful punch had punctured her duodenum, necessitating surgical repair. The scars on her body mirrored the deep wounds she carried within. Caught up in her story and deeply wanting to help her, I let go of my weariness and my desire to get home.

Apparently, her husband had threatened to take the kids away if she decided to leave, and moreover, should she stand up and face that risk, she would have nowhere to go. She could not sacrifice her children even if it meant surrendering herself. She was a hostage in her own home. She felt cornered. In her mind the only visible exit was to end her life. She revealed a haunting aspect of her past that has lingered in my thoughts for years. With a heavy tone, she shared, "Even as a kid, I always felt the desire to end it all."

A profound pause followed, as if she was reliving the tumultuous moments of her life. Struggling to articulate her feelings, she hauntingly chuckled with tears still running down her cheeks and said, "When I was ten, every time it rained, I would just go out and stand in the rain."

Another pause ensued, and then, almost in a whisper, as if she was still trying to hide from someone, she added, "If I cried inside the house, trouble would find me. Rain was my escape. It washed away my tears in the rain. No one ever knew."

Ten years young then, and the only comfort she found was hiding her fear and pain, and the only solace was imagining how she might end her life.

Her words painted a heartbreaking picture of a young soul silently grappling with immense pain, bent with the weight of grief, opaque amid the external elements and invisible to nearly everyone around her. Grief has a transformative power, shaping us in ways that are profound and often bending us until we break. The presence of prolonged, perhaps seemingly inescapable grief represents a failure on multiple fronts. It forces those of us who have chosen to become

"If I cried inside the house, trouble would find me. Rain was my escape. It washed away my tears in the rain.

healers to acknowledge that despite our efforts, certain scars may never fully fade. This young version of herself, marked by her experiences, was destined to carry the burden throughout her life. It's a painful truth that while interventions can mitigate the intensity of the pain, eradicating it entirely remains an elusive goal.

I could relate to her personal revelation about childhood abuse. I, too, had been molested for years as a child. These cycles break you, and one can never be whole again. Our shared history added another layer to my understanding of the long-lasting impact of such trauma. The wounds inflicted during those formative years are profound and often irrevocable, leaving an indelible mark on one's psyche, body, and soul.

Recognizing and addressing the pervasive and enduring effects of childhood abuse becomes imperative in fostering empathy and advocating for support systems that acknowledge the complexity of healing from such experiences. Poignant reflection on the shortcomings in mental health crisis support within healthcare highlights a critical issue that has far-reaching consequences. The lack of adequate resources for conditions such as anxiety, depression, and schizophrenia contribute to a disturbing rise in suicides, homelessness, and crime.

The pervasive stigma surrounding mental health further exacerbates the problem, deterring individuals from seeking help. Even for those who do seek assistance, discrimination against people with mental illness adds an additional layer of difficulty to their journey. The heartbreaking, profound failure by both family and society underscores the systemic challenges in addressing mental health issues.

In the immediate term, the fallout from the abuse she had suffered mostly in silence was misunderstood by many and openly ignored. She simply wanted something to take the pain away. This young woman's plea for a prescription to alleviate her pain reflected her desperate need for understanding and support. As she showed no signs of "medical" conditions needing treatment, following the expected protocols I had no choice but to clear her medically and move her into the care of the hospital psychiatrists. Under their management, she spent a few more days in the hospital, and in a week, she was discharged "home."

Two months later she hanged herself and died.

We failed her. Tragically, her death highlights the devastating consequences of inadequate mental health care. It reinforces the urgency for comprehensive and compassionate mental health support systems that address not only the symptoms but also the broader societal and systemic factors contributing to mental health challenges.

Every person lost underscores the collective responsibility to strive for more effective and empathetic approaches to mental health care. Every death demonstrates the need for a healthcare system that recognizes the inherent humanity and vulnerability of all who enter it. I still remember my patient's last words before I left her room that night: "My family failed me, society failed me, no one cares, and you people just write me a Xanax and go away."

She was right, of course. We doctors are quick with our prescription pads and short with our words and time. We don't have good systems in place to help people like this young woman.

If you are someone having chest pain, you call the paramedics or go to the hospital. But if you are thinking of committing suicide, one of the few choices for most is to call the suicide prevention hotline, 988, a number very few people even know about and one that was only voted into law in 2020. If you call 911, you may or may not get the help you need because those responding are trained to treat medical emergencies, not mental health crises or to offer suicide prevention tactics.

Should you receive outreach at all, even within emergency medical services and healthcare generally, there remain frequent stigmas attached to those seeking help and a limited numbers of professionals with the proper experience to provide the expertise needed. We have Band-Aids available—three days of involuntary hospital admission, psych transfers, Xanax, lithium—but not enough, not enough at all for mental health.

Similarly, there is a severe lack of support services in schools, and too often when children are encouraged to share their insecurities, they are marginalized, and in many cases they are bullied. An adult equivalent exists in most workplaces. Simply discussing someone's concerns about mental health is uncomfortable for nearly all people. And certainly, nearly all of us are ill equipped to be any real help. Public information campaigns have had limited effectiveness, and while some of the perceptions of mental health problems are changing, it is slow change that flows against the primary current.

An underlying reality is that when it comes to caring for illness, the medical establishment is far more adept at healing the brain than we are at healing the mind. We simply are better at taking action on neurological and physical maladies like treating the clogged brain vessels of stroke victims, even at educating for stroke prevention. We devote so much effort to repairing the brain but neglect to heal the mind.

Like all systemic issues, widespread, meaningful change is evasive, and very few offer the systemic approaches required. Until we have significant government reforms and funding available, these sad, harsh realities will not change. As a country, our resources are disproportionately allocated more toward procedural medicine with less attention to intellectual medicine. I am certain change is coming, especially after COVID-19, and I am hopeful more change is to come. Culturally, as evidenced with prominent athletes and other high-profile individuals now speaking openly about their mental health struggles, we seem a society poised for changing perceptions. A crack in the armor is forming. The circumstances and societal reluctance to face the problems that kept so many silent—so many dancing alone in the rain—are beginning to change.

I can't bring my patient back. But her example forced me to reconsider what success truly means in healthcare. Is it just about treating symptoms, or should we measure success by our ability to provide comprehensive, compassionate care that addresses the whole person?

There are moments when you may not have all the answers or even good news to share, but it's crucial for the patient to feel your presence and support. When a storm is raging outside, you may not be able to stop the rain or calm the winds, but simply offering shelter can make all the difference. It's not always about having the perfect solution; it's about being someone they can rely on, rain or shine.

It's true for the guy who shows up in the ER with chest pain who, beyond wanting the pain to end, wants the peace of mind that he's not having a heart attack. It's even true for the patient with end-stage brain cancer. I can't tell them they will be fine, but I can offer them peace of mind by being honest with them and telling them, "This is where we are, here's what you can expect, and we are in this thing together."

It's more than marking the checkboxes that the test results are complete and putting in orders for chemo or hospice. Cultivating resilience in both healthcare providers and patients requires us to invest in this deeper level of care. It's about fostering hope even in the most challenging circumstances.

We've gotten quite good at taking care of our patients' organs, but we do not invest in their souls. This is in part true because our system does not invest in the things that don't bring in revenue, and peace of mind does not generate income, at least not directly. This is true of virtually every vulnerable population. I speak of these failures through the lens of healthcare, for that is the world I know. It is the world many who suffer from conditions like PTSD and other trauma-based mental health conditions logically come to for help.

Both the causes that led this young woman to our psychiatric ward, like the impoverishment of solutions we were able to offer her (which, as she rightly accused us, ultimately contributed to her death), go far beyond healthcare. So long as we turn our backs on the larger societal ills that contribute to abuse and neglect, so long as our culture dismisses those who suffer from mental health conditions or pushes them to the street, so long as we treat any fellow human as less than human, we cannot offer individuals, or our collective society, any peace of mind.

It all starts with making human connections. Picture a yin-yang diagram. How the two parts are required to fill the circle. How they complement one another. When we connect with people, it takes both halves to make a whole. Only together is the puzzle complete.

Recognizing our commonality, even with strangers, is the first step, not just toward making better connections but toward coming to know one another in ways that we might learn to embrace one another, even trust each other. It begins with wishing to heal minds as well as brains. It commences with recognizing that acting on the means to heal minds includes those in healthcare but does not end there; it is in all of us, whether we are counselors or teachers, artists, or soldiers, and it is required of us regardless of our religion or our race, our nationality, or our culture.

It starts with creating one-on-one connections. By wanting to know my patient's background, in wishing to hear her story, I was able to learn about her past and about the conditions that contributed to her desire to end her life. But, of course, that was not enough. No miracle happened that day. Her circumstances did not change simply because I took time to listen to her.

But if I keep trying to make connections with others, and if you do, maybe one of us will reach one person who would have given up had we not. I encounter the same frequency of disconnect in my work as a CEO as I do as a doctor. Maybe it's that employee who doesn't seem to mesh with the team. Maybe the frustration faced by an angry customer is really the fault of miscommunication. Possibly the underperforming team member just isn't in the position that best fits their individual strengths, a fact we can't know unless we connect and we care.

The decisions we make as leaders always have consequences, sometimes big and sometimes small, and they always have impact on people's lives, but they are seldom fatal. We can, however, learn from those leaders whose decisions can have dire consequences, not just medical professionals but those in the military and law enforcement, pilots, and others. The larger the stakes, the more care we must take, and the more complicated the circumstance. The more we learn to follow our conscience and think about the human consequences of the smaller decisions we regularly make, the better position we are in to tackle the big decisions.

You or I won't solve treatment for those with depression or put a magical stop to abusive behavior. We won't solve homelessness or end racism, but we can each do our part. It starts by conditioning ourselves to be sympathetic beings. If we can find mental peace within ourselves, we will be far more successful in doing our part in helping someone else find that place within themselves.

What might I do differently if I could go back in time? How might I have been a better doctor for this patient? For all my patients? How might I be a better boss for my employees? Such introspection is a starting place. All I know for sure is this: I would wish no one such despair that they seek refuge in the rain, hiding their tears from a world too blind to see.

I cannot bring that woman back from the desperation that led to her suicide, but perhaps, if we work together, we might help a different young woman believe she has reason to hope.

While I couldn't save that young woman, her story fuels my resilience. It drives me to continually seek better ways to instill hope in patients and in those who care for them, redefining success in terms of our ability to truly see and care for each individual.

The more we learn to follow our conscience and think about the human consequences of the small decisions we regularly make, the better position we are in to tackle the big decisions.

INTERSECTIONS

Walking along the beach, I noticed two sets of footprints etched in the sand, crossing each other's path. The people who left them were nowhere to be seen, yet their fleeting presence lingered. These imprints told a quiet story—two lives on separate journeys intersecting briefly, leaving behind a trace of connection before continuing on their way.

CHAPTER 4

Invisible People: We Are More Than the Uniforms We Wear

The true measure of a man is how he treats someone who can do him absolutely no good.
—SAMUEL JOHNSON

Let's talk about something close to my heart: the "little people." No, I am not talking about Hobbits or garden gnomes. I mean people who are invisible. And by *invisible*, I'm not talking about the "I see dead people" ghosts from *The Sixth Sense* either. I'm referring to the unsung heroes who keep our world spinning while often staying invisible to society's eye. I am talking about those people we *make* invisible—those who clean our floors, deliver our food, empty our trash—those who do the jobs that most of us overlook. A lot of these jobs are probably where some of us got our start.

During the early days of my own journey, long before the white coat and the stethoscope, my world was dominated by the hum of a carpet cleaner and the faint smell of detergent and bleach that seemed to cling to everything. It was a time of humility and hustle, of invisible labor that many walked over—quite literally—without a second thought.

After a full day of assisting in clinical research, every evening as I donned my plain uniform—a simple set of overalls that marked both my occupation and my invisibility—I stepped into a role that society deemed lowly. People rarely looked beyond the machinery and the noise it produced to see the person operating it. There I was, maneuvering through offices and halls, becoming part of the backdrop of others' busy lives. They shuffled papers and answered phones, glancing briefly with a nod or a fleeting smile, if at all. It's human nature; people pass others all the time without showing recognition that they have encountered another human being.

I remember many evenings working late in a vast, empty office while the sunset cast long shadows across the carpet I was cleaning, shadows that seemed to echo my feelings of smallness. Despite the solitude of the job, I found a sense of importance in my work. Not the kind of importance that comes with accolades or recognition, but the quiet pride of making spaces clean and welcoming.

It was in those moments, with the steady noise of the rotating brush filling the air, invisible to those immediately around me, that I allowed myself to think of my family, my friends, and my colleagues—those who saw beyond the uniform. To them, I was not just the background character in someone else's scene; I was a protagonist in my own right. I was studying, aiming for a future that seemed so distant yet drove me to push through each day.

Feeling invisible in my uniform taught me a profound lesson about seeing others. It embedded in me a sense of empathy and recognition for all forms of work and the people who perform them.

Every role carries its weight and worth. Every person harbors a story deserving of respect.

Over time, I became convinced that if we focus more on the roles we play rather than obsessing over the titles we seek, we might better appreciate each person's contribution in the grand theater of life. These days, I get a certain satisfaction from introducing myself as a "fake CEO." It keeps me grounded, reminding me it's just another role—and it's my way of calling out those who demand respect based solely on titles and hierarchies.

Now, as I walk through hospital corridors adorned in a white coat or a sports jacket (another uniform) that may (or may not) get me some respect, I carry with me the lessons I learned from those carpet-cleaning days. I make it a point to acknowledge nearly everyone, no matter their job. From the cleaners who keep our spaces pristine to the nurses who work tirelessly by my side, I see them. For I know too well the feeling of being invisible, and I strive to ensure that those around me never feel that way.

Every person harbors a story deserving of respect.

I often emphasize that no matter how skilled a neurosurgeon may be, their expertise is moot if the cleaners have not adequately prepared the operating room. A successful surgery hinges on a clean, sterile environment. In the same vein, the grandest designs of an architect would be futile without the truck drivers, often traveling for days, who transport the supplies required to build what once only existed on a paper or the dedicated laborers who prepare the groundwork and tie the rebar embedded in the building's foundation. Ultimately, recognizing the multiple levels of labor required to achieve desired outcomes underscores the fundamental truth that we are all interconnected. We exist in a network of relationships, each reflecting or casting shadows upon one another. By the end of the day, the life message repeats itself, and we are all related to each other.

The invisible chapter of my life, humbling and often hard, shaped not just my career but my beliefs. It taught me that importance is not granted by a uniform or a title but by how we treat others and the integrity we bring to our work, no matter the task at hand. It is a lesson I hope to pass on, a reminder that we are part of a larger whole, each one vital, none truly invisible. The hierarchies our cultures have constructed are constructs.

We exist in a network of relationships, each reflecting or casting shadows upon one another. By the end of the day, the life message repeats itself, and we are all related to each other.

Rather than divide people by their perceived "value" to us or their place in a manufactured hierarchy, would we not be wise to recognize that we are all interdependent? Understanding that roles and perspectives are more important than titles has shaped my approach to leadership in my current role as a healthcare executive, leading a company composed of highly educated professionals, each of whom relies on collaboration and mutual support to achieve our shared goals. None of us arrived at our professions on the same path. And none of us can walk our current path alone.

We often overlook "invisible" people, not out of malice but because we are so caught up in our own lives. Think about it: When was the last time you thanked the delivery person who brought your dinner or the janitor who makes sure your workspace is spotless? These folks might be on the fringes of society, but they are the backbone of our daily routines.

There is humongous value in the power of acknowledgment. I can quote *Harvard Business Review* or *Journal of Business Studies* findings that employees who feel recognized and valued are significantly more productive.[4] They exist by the score. This is not rocket science, folks! A simple "Thank you!" or a genuine smile can truly brighten someone's day. Moreover, we do not need countless studies to tell us this; if we could all just embrace a bit more humanity, humility, and common sense, the world would be a better place. We have no control over others to be kind, but everyone has an ability to be kind to everyone.

Remember, there are souls who drift like shadows to many, yet to others they are light itself—indispensable. Life is full of twists and turns, and sometimes we are the ones who need that kind smile or helping hand; be the first to extend your hand. By acknowledging the invisible heroes around us, we create a ripple effect of kindness and compassion. Who knows? By showing appreciation, you might just make someone's day—or even change their life.

Visible Invisibility

In the US, we like to believe that we do not have a caste system, so much so that we view ourselves as superior to places like India, where in 2024 there are 272 million people seen as belonging to the Dalit caste, commonly referred to as "the Untouchables" because they are not allowed to drink from the same wells, attend the same temples, use the same cups, or wear shoes in the presence of an upper-caste person.[5] Because they are viewed as impure, Dalits are subject to public ridicule,

4 Shawn Achor, "How Positive Employee Recognition Increases Engagement and Productivity," *Harvard Business Review* (January–February 2012), https://hbr.org/2012/01/positive-intelligence; Adrian Gostick and Chester Elton, *The Carrot Principle: How the Best Managers Use Recognition to Engage Their Employees, Retain Talent, and Drive Performance* (Simon and Schuster, 2007).

5 "The Present and Future of Dalit Politics," Civilsdaily, October 25, 2023, https://www.civilsdaily.com/news/the-present-and-future-of-dalit-politics/.

harassed, openly beaten, and abused, all with impunity. Similarly, the Makranis of Pakistan, descendants of African slaves brought to the region centuries ago, live within the shadows of Karachi, bound by a legacy of servitude that still haunts them.

Their history is etched in the dark shades of their skin and the distinctive features that set them apart from the rest of the population. In a society that often measures worth through lineage and complexion, the Makranis remain on the periphery, struggling against deep-rooted prejudices that have kept them from attaining true equality.

Yet are we in the US so far removed from operating within a de facto caste system? In the heart of our bustling cities, amid the shadows of skyscrapers and the cacophony of busy streets, exists a segment of the population often overlooked or purposefully turned away from—people so invisible that some do not label them human. Easier to call them bums or freeloaders; easier to believe they live on our streets, in our parks, and on the fringes of industrial zones by choice or that they all suffer untreatable psychological disorders. Is such treatment really so different than formally labeling others "untouchable"?

These individuals are the most vulnerable members of society, often hidden in plain sight, withstanding the worst of urban plight and inner-city decay. One of the things we fail to see is that these invisible people make up a diverse group, each with unique challenges and stories. Some tag them as homeless people; others call them displaced or unhoused—descriptors I see as euphemisms meant to offer us a more palatable, scoured image of a reality that we find disturbing. Often the most visible among the invisible, these individuals live without the basic security of a stable shelter. Their visibility in public spaces starkly contrasts with their societal invisibility; by drawing attention to the stark contrast between their visible presence in public spaces and their societal invisibility, one can shed light on the struggles faced by marginalized communities, advocating for more recognition, understanding, and inclusion in both public discourse and policymaking.

I met one homeless man, "Freddie Socks," for the first time a decade ago as he was sitting next to a building on the street on the outskirts of downtown Tampa while I was practicing street medicine. He sat in a place where the hustle of city life softens just enough for you to hear your own thoughts. He was a fixture on the streets where the Pioneer Medical Foundation would conduct clinics for the homeless. Freddie, in his late fifties but bearing the marks of a man much older, carried the weight of the world in his tired eyes and weathered face. He was an imposing figure, a mountain of a man whose beard could put ZZ Top to shame—thick, long, white, and commanding attention just like the man himself.

A tangle of neurotransmitters collided with his faith, twisting it into a storm that blurred reality and belief—leaving him grappling with the disorienting grip of schizophrenia, whispering unseen challenges and shaping his reality in ways difficult for you and me to grasp. Most of the time I would find him having a thoughtful dialogue with an imaginary friend, deep in somber discussion, simultaneously speaking and listening to himself as if immersed in an internal rhythm of conversation.

Freddie had not always lived on the streets. Over time, as I became a familiar presence, we came to know each other well enough to talk regularly. He told me that decades ago he was a carpenter, skilled with his hands and proud of his work. He crafted furniture that was not just functional but beautiful, imbued with the kind of care that comes from true passion. As I got to know him, I learned about the man he used to be—a man who loved the smell of freshly cut wood and the satisfaction of creating something from nothing.

His tales were scattered, often lost in the tangle of his thoughts, but they were glimpses into a life that once was full of potential and regular joy. But life, as it often does, threw curveballs that no one could have predicted. His mental health began to deteriorate in his thirties, shadows creeping into his mind that no amount of daylight could dispel.

As his condition worsened, the stigma associated with mental illness coupled with his increasing difficulty to maintain steady employment gradually nudged him toward the fringes of society. The safety nets failed one by one—no sufficient medical intervention, no family support to lean on. Over time, Freddie found himself living on the streets, marginalized not just by his mental condition but by a community that often looked away from a visible invisibility they would rather not see.

Each time I visited that part of town, Freddie recognized me. His eyes lit up briefly, revealing a spark of recognition that pierced the fog of his daily struggles. We formed an unlikely acquaintance, one founded on small exchanges and consistent interactions. Despite his hardships, Freddie had peculiarities that made him uniquely him. He had an aversion to new clothing and would politely decline any offer except for socks—hence Freddie "Socks." Those, he cherished. "Keeps the feet happy," he would say with a faint smile, a reminder of simpler comforts that brought him some measure of peace.

The last time I saw Freddie, it was an unusually cold December morning. He was particularly quiet, the usual spark in his eyes dimmed to a mere flicker. He accepted a new pair of socks, his hands trembling as they brushed against the soft fabric. We spoke little, but our exchange was a comfort in its familiarity. A week later, I learned that Freddie had passed away quietly in his sleep, tucked into an alcove he called his "winter spot."

I heard the news during one of my Pioneer Medical Foundation service projects. Learning of his death hit me harder than I expected. Freddie's life and passing were a stark reminder of how easily individuals can slip through the cracks of our society, unseen and often unremembered. I wish we could have done more for him, that his final years could have been spent in warmth and dignity rather than in the shadows of indifference.

Freddie's story, marked by both the joy of his early years and the sorrow of his decline, lingers as an anchor to the complexities of human life and the profound impact of societal neglect. In every shadowed gaze and weathered face, there's a story aching to be known, a life woven deeply with quiet importance.

In my journey, I have encountered many individuals who remind me of Freddie, though their stories and struggles vary widely. These "Freddies" might appear as single mothers sitting on dimly lit sidewalks desperately trying to forget their lives by smoking crack while their innocent children play beside them. My hearts stops for a bit looking at these kids, and I wonder if they ever really had a chance. Yet I also wonder, *Who were these women before their addiction?*

I remember a former aerospace engineer found under the sparse shade of a tree in Hyde Park, barely clothed and far removed from his past career. What was his story? Who had he left behind? What of the runaway teens who flee abusive homes, finding themselves swallowed up by the urban landscape where they are dangerously exposed and deprived of any stability or nurturing? Who could they have become had they not suffered at the hands of another?

Every person living on the street has a unique, individual story. All involve heartache in one form or another. They are as diverse as the lives of those gathered around a conference table during a corporate meeting or those surrounding you in a busy restaurant. The only constant between Freddie, an addicted mother, a fallen engineer, a teenager exchanging sexual favors for food, and all their street companions is the stigma that clings to their existence—a mark as debilitating as any physical ailment.

The heartbreak I have felt in coming to know individuals suffering such stigma only deepened when I have tried to help create the possibility of change in their lives. Overwhelmed by their numbers and the depth of their needs, those trying to help them encounter harsh decisions. I have, through the Pioneer Medical Foundation, worked with other agencies and nonprofits that face the experience of making impossible decisions that directly impact human lives.

I decided quite early while writing this book that I will not talk much about my healthcare companies, but I would like to talk a little about the Pioneer Medical Foundation in Tampa Bay, Florida. In 2015 I called Dr. Khan and suggested that we need to do something for our community, reminding him of our shared belief that we should give back to the community and the country that made us who we are today. We decided to take healthcare to where the people are. Initially on foot and later with mobile healthcare vans, through health fairs and finally with permanent clinics, our mission is to provide free healthcare services to the underserved, including the homeless, refugees, and uninsured adults.

The Pioneer Medical Foundation now operates several outreach clinic sites in impoverished neighborhoods, homeless shelters, transitional group housing, churches, and community centers. It provides a range of services, including clinics for the underinsured, specialty consultations, medication assistance, and hygiene supplies. These services are delivered through a mobile medical unit that travels throughout several counties in the Tampa Bay area. As we decided never to take monetary donations from outside our parent organization, we were often criticized that we would never grow. My usual response is that we are only trying to fix what we can. Most crucial is the philosophy that our compassion for people should not be terminated on the basis of their insurance card.

During one of my discussions in the early stages of setting up the foundation, a school superintendent serving on the board of a homeless shelter provided an example of the kinds of impossible choices they regularly faced. It is because of such difficult decisions that homeless shelters must have very precise policies, because all of them encounter more requests for assistance than they have the means to fulfill. Consider the case of two sixteen-year-old girls, one living in her undrivable car but who has a job that provides her with income sufficient enough to purchase food, although insufficient for her to afford traditional housing; the other living on the balcony of her abusive father's apartment.

Is the latter girl "homeless"? Is the girl who sleeps in her car in greater need? The first girl, who lives in a car, meets a strict definition of homeless. Her counterpart may not, for her father's presence and his balcony can be considered shelter. On the other hand, as a victim of his abuse, wouldn't it be safer to get her into a different environment? The girl living in the car got the spot; the girl on the balcony didn't. In the real world, we must make such heart-wrenching, impossible choices. Such choices are not just administrative; they are deeply conflicting at times, and they leave lasting scars on the conscience.

What most of us fail to remember—or openly turn away from—are simplest truths: Both girls have names; they are someone's child; somewhere, at some time, other people have loved them, and quite likely someone still does. The invisible people are our neighbors, friends, and distant family members pushed to the margins of our world. Recognizing their humanity is the first step. We must see them not just as victims or cases to be managed but as individuals with stories, hopes, and dreams.

Resources will remain finite. Circumstances will remain complex. We cannot help everyone even if our heart wishes us to. What we can do is help people with whom we can connect. We can make differences within the scale of our time and resources. We can recognize that the donation of our time and perhaps whatever expertise we may have is of far greater value than our money. If we could fix homelessness with money alone, there would be no girls living on balconies or in cars, and Freddie Socks would be sprinting in Nikes.

I am reminded of "The Starfish Story" (as it is commonly referenced; it was officially first published as a sixteen-page essay titled "The Starfish Thrower"), by Loren Eiseley, which I read decades ago, but Stephen Covey also used Eiseley's example in his book *The 7 Habits of Highly Effective People*. The story illustrates the impact of individual actions and is often cited as a metaphor for making a difference, no matter how small. It is a story about a man walking on a beach that is riddled with countless starfish. He encounters another man, who is one by one throwing starfish back into the sea.

"What are you doing?" the former asks. "There are millions of starfish. You throwing them back one at a time isn't going to make a difference."

The other man picks up another starfish and returns it to the ocean and says, "I made a difference for that one."

That's where we start. We get to know our own Freddies. We may or may not be able to make a difference in their lives, but it is worth trying. Every small victory is worth celebrating. Here's just one example. When the Pioneer Medical Foundation holds a health fair, we not only get hundreds of volunteers; we get them from every walk of life. This allows us to provide so many things that homeless people need, far beyond the stereotypical vision of a health fair where participants get rudimentary medical screenings.

Our version includes services like barbers, manicurists, and mobile showers, knowing that something common to all people is the belief that when we look good, we feel better about ourselves. We assemble a huge collection of donated clothing. We bring in dentists, surgeons, podiatrists, psychiatrists, counselors, pulmonologists, pharmacists, and spiritual advisors. We offer free medicine. We extract decayed teeth. We offer invitations to rehabilitation services. We serve everyone in attendance a meal prepared by the staff of high-end restaurants.

At one recent fair, I met a homeless man who said he had a job interview later in the day. He took advantage of what we offered, took a shower, got a haircut, and selected a nice shirt and tie. At a later foundation event, he gleefully reported that he got the job for which he had interviewed.[6]

Creating Visibility

Change takes place one person at a time. It can start small, though, of course, extending compassion means more than temporary relief; it involves advocating for systemic changes that address the root causes of homelessness and marginalization. It is about creating pathways that lead back to society, offering more than just survival—providing dignity, support, and a real chance to thrive.

The small steps we can each take always start close to home. When you act on such principles, life often has a way of humbling you. Recently, I posed a question to a small group within my company

---

6 If you would like to learn more about the Pioneer Medical Foundation, here is an introductory video. This is just one of numerous videos the foundation has prepared to capture some of the work to which we are dedicated.

asking about what they think of when they hear the phrase *invisible people*. Many responses echoed the sentiments I have shared. However, one response particularly struck me.

It came from a young woman in her twenties, someone I have known since she was a teenager and who had started as a receptionist. I watched her grow personally and professionally, and now she is completing her MBA. This young woman quietly admitted, "I am that invisible person."

Her words took me aback and left me feeling disappointed in myself. This made me realize another one of my blind spots. How could I know this young woman so well and not recognize that she felt invisible? How could I not understand what such invisibility meant to her? Perhaps I had contributed to that perception in my interactions with her. Clearly, I had a perception removed from reality. We always need to ask questions and hear the answers.

Who might view themselves as invisible in your life? Do you see all the people upon whom you rely? Do you acknowledge that they matter to you? When is the last time you did something kind for a stranger—or for that matter for the invisible person you see every day? The least we can do is try.

JOY

I saw this man sitting on Charles Bridge in Prague. His smile got my attention when I took this photograph. I saw him living in the moment, with a carefree attitude that revealed freedom and fulfillment.

CHAPTER 5
Kindness: A Mutant Gene

I have found that it is the small everyday deed of ordinary folks that keep the darkness at bay. Small acts of kindness and love.
—J. R. R. TOLKIEN, THE LORD OF THE RINGS

"You are a mutant," I playfully declared to my best friend.

My abrupt statement lingered in the crisp winter air. It was late at night, and we were standing under the muted glow of a streetlamp outside his home. Our conversation centered around good and evil, how some people forgive so easily and others get so engulfed by resentment that they become like color-blind people living in a monochromatic world. These individuals are blind to appreciating the goodness in life, and they become universally skeptical.

I was nineteen then. Our friendship thrived because of our shared love of books and chess. He, far more intellectually adept than I was, loved math and eventually charted a course as an actuarial mathematician. We used to hang out a few times a week at his home. His house, just a few minutes' walk away, became a sanctuary for our chess battles and literary explorations. The fun of those interactions, now bathed in the nostalgia of time gone by, still resonates in my memories. When I think about all that now, the chess and the bookish conversations sound really geeky, but the friendship never does.

He was my first best friend even though we were so different. The threads of our personalities were interwoven harmoniously but remained distinct. A born introvert, he found comfort in the quiet recesses of his thoughts. While I was far from an introvert, I moved through life with a blend of boldness and a certain reckless curiosity—often diving in headfirst, a little clueless, a little careless, but always ready to take risks just to see where they'd lead. Despite these differences, our connection was symbiotic, each trait complementing the other in a dance of mutual respect. His intentional nature provided a sturdy anchor to my more spontaneous tendencies. I would plunge into every trouble with an almost carefree enthusiasm, and in those moments, he lived vicariously through my experiences. He found a certain joy watching me navigate the unpredictable currents of life, a joy that he experienced while observing from the sidelines. As the chapters of our lives unfolded, the symbiosis persisted for a long time. I continued to be the one with stories to tell, and he the one with lessons to impart.

That night, as the clock ticked toward the early hours, our conversation tapered toward evolution, a topic of interest to both of us. This was the kind of terrain our conversations navigated, although sometimes with a modicum of wariness, for growing up as a Muslim, evolution was not a topic I was allowed to believe in, and I always felt a slight guilt discussing such forbidden subjects, no matter how intriguing I find this topic to this day. I think that night could have been the start of my lifelong questioning of dogma.

Our conversation moved on. We were discussing what one should do when faced with adversity. I reflected on the complexities. "Should we seek a ray of light in the darkness, react with anger, or simply forgive?" I pondered aloud.

Expanding on the idea, I turned to my friend and shared, "I want you to take this as a compliment when I say that you are a mutant because you are so kind."

It was simply a statement of truth; he was one of the kindest people I knew, in a league with my idols. In this observation, I sought to convey the uniqueness and rarity of his kindness, a quality that stood out like an anomaly in the face of life's challenges. Mine was a contemplation on the intricate choices life presents.

As I delved into my belief, I explained that human evolution, shaped by the struggle for survival, had slowly crafted one intrinsic trait—survival at all cost. I suggested that kindness, often overlooked in the survival narrative, was a form of mutation—an exceptional quality that set species and individuals apart. In a world where the instinct for survival often leaned toward self-preservation, kindness emerged as a distinctive trait, a subtle rebellion against the harshness of existence.

I want you to take this as a compliment when I say that you are a mutant because you are so kind.

My ancestors probably climbed over everyone present to escape danger, hurt and maimed others to get a meal. We were programmed to survive. It didn't matter what the cost was for survival; the choices were limited: become endangered or morph into a predator. *Homo sapiens* even took out Neanderthals as well as other archaic hominoids in a relatively (in evolutionary terms) short amount of time. Unfortunately, those evolutionary instincts are as present now as they were then, even if our methodologies for ensuring survival have grown more nuanced.

I was trying to express to my friend my belief that somewhere during all this chaos, some individuals evolved with a mutant "kindness gene." Maybe it is the same gene shared by Mother Teresa, Nelson Mandela, Pope John Paul II, or Abdul Sattar Edhi. Somewhere in time we learned that life is a little more than fulfilling our own needs or wants. Somewhere we learned there could be value in remaining hungry and sharing a meal with a stranger. *Homo sapiens* all of a sudden became "human."

I remember that I took a brief pause during our conversation and then shared with my friend, "In this unjust world, what keeps me going is one steadfast belief. I try to forgive those who do wrong, because in the end, they are only being 'human,' true to their evolutionary imperative. On the other hand, if someone is kind—now *that* is something to celebrate. We should be grateful for these rare individuals. They are the mutants, carrying an uncommon kindness gene."

Highlighting the significance of kindness, I spoke of it as a rarity, a mutation in human evolution. Those who possess this "mutant kindness gene" become beacons in the darkness, individuals worthy of celebration and gratitude. In the span of the complicated, intricate process of human evolution, the emergence of a kindness gene stands as a remarkable catalyst for societal progress. This genetic anomaly, manifesting as an innate propensity for compassion and altruism, has not only shaped individual relationships but played a pivotal role in the survival and advancement of our species. Is this really fiction?

> Those who possess this "mutant kindness gene" become beacons in the darkness, individuals worthy of celebration and gratitude.

This exploration of kindness as a mutant gene intertwines science, sociology, and anthropology to offer a compelling perspective on how acts of goodwill have not only shaped our past but continue to influence the trajectory of human evolution. It was not a surprise to me, then, that with time, science actually found the genesis of kindness. A study conducted by scientists at Oregon State University, published in *Proceedings of the National Academy of Sciences*, explored a variation that was linked to the body's receptor gene of oxytocin, a love hormone.[7]

They conducted an experiment with twenty-three couples already tested for GG, AG, or AA genotypes. Individuals homozygous for the G allele (GG genotype) of the oxytocin receptor tend to be more "prosocial," defined by researchers as the ability to behave in a way that benefits another person. In contrast, the carriers of the A version of the gene (AG or AA genotypes) tend to have a higher risk of autism as well as self-reported lower levels of positive emotions, empathy, and parental sensitivity.

By comparison, oxytocin has been significantly linked with social affiliation and reduction in stress. It is a peptide made in the hypothalamus and has targets all over the body and the brain. It is best known for its role in female reproduction and is associated with social recognition, pair bonding, dampened negative emotional responses, trust, and love.

In the study, the twenty-three romantic couples were videotaped while one of the partners described a time of suffering in their lives. The other half of the couple and their physical, nonverbal reactions were the focal point of the study. Groups of complete strangers viewed the videos. The observers were asked to rate the person on traits such

---

7 "The Kindness of Strangers: Caring and Trust Linked to Genetic Variation," Oregon State University Newsroom, November 14, 2011, https://news.oregonstate.edu/news/kindness-strangers-caring-and-trust-linked-genetic-variation.

as how kind, trustworthy, and caring they thought the person was based on just twenty seconds of silent video. These observations were then compared to the genotype data.

Out of the ten people who were marked by the neutral observer as "most prosocial," six carried the GG genotype associated with the oxytocin receptor; of the ten people who were marked as "least trusted," nine were carriers of the A version of the gene.[8] The people carrying an A version of the gene were viewed as less kind, trustworthy, and caring toward their partners in the video. Researchers concluded that a genetic makeup may have an impact on how people behave and demonstrate levels of empathy, trust, and loving behaviors. Then there is 23andMe. I got a notification from the site Kindness Is in Our Genes and their collaboration with Kindness.org to further genetic research on kindness, altruism, and empathy. I will confess that when I read this, I gloated a little bit. Probably my "unkind" genes were acting out.

I am not trying to create behavior parallels with Darwinian principles as one theory, as we know there are so many collective variables that define us as an individual, as a collective, as a community, or as a nation. All I know is that kindness and cooperation stand the test of time, making us more resilient and better equipped to overcome challenges, ultimately leading to us as a whole person.

In the end, I said the following to my friend that night: "It makes it easier for me to forgive and forget when faced with adversarial people, because I believe their behavior is not their fault. They simply may not have the kindness gene. But more than making me forgive those who don't display kindness, the genetic explanation immensely helps me appreciate the people carrying the traits that demonstrate extraordinary acts of kindness. In my mind, they are the true X-Men."

---

8 Ibid.

As the years have passed, I find myself reminiscing about those times, about the shared dreams and the unspoken promises of lifelong friendship. At the time, our brotherly bond of friendship felt like an everlasting flame, flickering in the gentle breeze of shared interest and passions. The declaration that day of "you are a mutant" continues to echo.

In the act of writing, there are moments when the weight of one's words carry a subtle undercurrent of hypocrisy. It's an internal dialogue that emerges and occasionally contradicts your own mind. The dichotomy between the words crafted and the emotions felt can create a dissonance, a discordant harmony that is hard to ignore. Feeling the hypocrisy as one writes becomes a poignant reminder of the intricate nature of self-expression and the continuous journey toward authenticity. It is in navigating this nuanced terrain that the true depth and honesty of one's voice can emerge.

Ironically and regretfully, my friend and I drifted apart. We have not connected for thirty years. One of my regrets is that I could have tried harder to bridge the gap of time and place. I should have tried harder to reach out. To do so would have been the smallest act of kindness. To lose a friend … now *that* is a real failure.

I learned from the distance that time wrought and have tried since then to understand all the other lifelong friends I have made. I try not to be fixated on what I believe but on understanding their beliefs first. As one of my friends often says to me, "Would you rather be happy or right?" I cannot get into a time machine or wish upon a ring and go back and prevent the thirty years of our absent friendship. But I can learn to be a better friend to others and to cherish the time I have in their company.

CELEBRATION

I saw my daughter jumping up and down by a fountain, carefree, full of energy, surrendering to unfiltered joy and enjoying the moment.

CHAPTER 6

Savoring Life's Moments: Finding Balance

The hardest thing to find in life is balance—especially the more success you have, the more you look to the other side of the gate. What do I need to stay grounded, in touch, in love, connected, emotionally balanced? Look within yourself.

—CÉLINE DION

I've shared some of my unpleasant memories of growing up, but if I left you only with visions of bullies or of families so poor they could not afford a prescription for an antibiotic, I have painted a vastly incomplete picture, one that is unfair and inaccurate of my life.

Those unpleasant things are true. But so is the joy I remember at sundown every evening during Eid, when people dress in their finest, brightest fabrics, basking in the celebratory spirit of fireworks and the festive atmosphere of a meal shared with my relatives and the communion experience being among people I love.

The idea of the Ramadan fasting period is to abstain from pleasure in order to grow spiritually. Then the breaking of the fast, the chance to eat a meal among family, enhances the day that has been spent in reflection and quiet. There is clarity and joy after sunset, sweetening the laughter of my young daughters, enhancing the glow of my beautiful wife's smile, strengthening the bond I have with my parents and siblings. The feelings are as moving and vivid as tending to a tree that has almost withered during a harsh winter. With patience and care, they nurture it back to life, and when spring finally arrives, the tree blooms even more beautifully than before, a quiet testament to resilience and hope.

What are your own fondest memories? Picture the familiar faces of your parents, the warmth of their presence shaping the earliest contours of your world. Recall the laughter and camaraderie shared with childhood friends, whose bonds felt unbreakable in the simplicity of those days when a swing or a slide held a promise of joy, when playing with friends could build a universe.

Close your eyes and rewind. Reflect on the joys of simple things. Journey back into the tapestry of your life, those jubilant memories and cherished interactions during exhilarating games of tag played with childhood companions, the lost echoes of innocent laughter, the hues of nostalgia, the small, trifling things that brought joy. Recall the exhilaration before a school trip, the eager excitement of buying school supplies for the approaching year, the moment you entered a toy store, that bubbly feeling before blowing out candles on a birthday treat, or the rush of joy before tearing the wrapping paper off a gift.

Revisit the warmth of love and protection found in a hug from your mother. Picture your grandparents. Smell the distinct aroma of a friend's backyard, recapture the fluttering excitement of your first crush, hear the old melodies that carry you to specific memories. Cherish anew the thrill of your favorite car ride or the freedom of letting your hand dance in the wind outside a car window. Transport yourself back into bubbling anticipation before the departure on a long-awaited vacation. Can you still recall what it was like to embrace a downpour without a care in the world, stomping in puddles, turning your face to the rain?

As we reflect, it becomes evident that these memories are the threads weaving the fabric of our past. Allow yourself the freedom to delve into those moments of joy, perhaps even jot them down. In revisiting such moments, we reconnect with the exhilarating and happy instances that shaped the foundation of who we are today. My wife often says, "One has to find happiness within; no one else can bring you happiness."

The other option is that you can choose to live only under the dark shades and find sanctuary in misery. Light and dark. Highlight and shadow. Our lives are never just one or the other. Life's not just sunshine and rainbows. Those moments of relief, rebellion, experiment, and sheer freedom? They're just as much a part of the fabric of life as the challenges and uncertainties. That's the beauty of it all—the messy, intricate, and wonderfully unpredictable journey we call life.

Life, my friend, is a river flowing between calm and turbulence, where joys share the stage with sorrows. Think about those setbacks that hit you square in the chest, the heartaches that left you breathless, the loves that slipped through your fingers like sand.

Remember the sting of bad grades, the weight of your own disappointing actions, and the times when others let you down (or you let someone down). Reflect on the bruises left by abuse, the hunger that gnaws, the struggles to make ends meet, the void left by lost loved ones, the painful end of relationships, the sharp pang of job insecurities, and the echo of unappreciated efforts.

And let's not forget the fractures—friendships breaking, rejections stinging, career choices that felt like dead ends. Consider the unmet expectations, the internal struggles to grasp your own capabilities, the battles with health, the opportunities that evaded you, and the bittersweet feeling of unfulfilled potential.

These, my friends, are not easy threads to weave into the fabric of life. They're the shadows, the darker hues that add depth and contrast to the canvas. Yet in their own way, they contribute to the intricate beauty of the whole masterpiece. It's the messy, complicated, and deeply profound nature of the journey we're all on. Without the lows, you can't truly appreciate the highs. Just like without darkness, the brilliance of light wouldn't dazzle us. It's the delicate blend of contrasts that makes life's story so rich.

But here's the real kicker—the most significant stumble isn't in facing sadness or darkness; it's in losing sight of the bigger picture. It's when we get stuck, tethered to the past, unable to look beyond our current circumstances. The true failure is in neglecting the chance to move forward, make amends, and carve out a path to success. We often trip over our own feet because we struggle to let go of what's holding us back. Here's where I'm waving the flag for embracing the positive.

Now, I'm not saying forget the past; that's not the play. What I'm rooting for is forgiveness—of ourselves and others. It's about learning from our stumbles, recognizing our inherent imperfections—our unique manufacturing defects. Because you know what? Imperfection is the spice of our existence, the part that makes us beautifully, authentically human. So, chin up, my friend. It's a journey, and the bumps and imperfections? They're what make it one heck of a ride.

We often trip over our own feet because we struggle to let go of what's holding us back.

I've attempted various methods to numb the pain when I fail, striving to forget those moments as if they never occurred. However, such efforts prove futile; these experiences resurface with a forceful resurgence, demanding acknowledgment and introspection. You can decide to drown yourself in self-pity or make a conscious decision to live an intentional life. Accept who you are. To be human is to err, right?

Memories play the role of both a friend and a trickster. Difficult memories are tricky things, but guess what? They fade with time. If every mom vividly remembered every second of the pain of childbirth, it's likely we would not have siblings. On the flip side, those cherished moments, the ones you want to hold on to forever—they're not immune either. Time has a way of gently smoothing out the edges.

Regrettably, earlier on, finding the sweet spot of balance was like trying to juggle flaming torches. Blame it on being driven, goal oriented, or maybe just fueled by the fear of falling short professionally. See, the tricky part is that balance isn't a one-size-fits-all deal. I used to throw around this term—*balance*—as if I had it all figured out.

Let me start by saying that finding balance in medicine is a constant struggle. It's a unique calling—demanding deep compassion, unyielding focus, and relentless dedication. Yet even in this relentless pursuit, balance is essential. It requires the ability to care for others while preserving your own well-being, to navigate the intensity of saving lives while staying grounded in your own humanity. Medicine demands everything, but it also teaches that without balance, even the strongest can falter.

Picture an old-fashioned balance scale; place the weights so that there is a 70/30 split. In our lives, what is the 30 percent weighing down one arm of the scale? Work. As a younger man, 70/30 was uncommon, with the heavy side of the scale dropping to the table with a thump. With the climb up the professional ladder, the higher you go, the lonelier you become as more responsibilities pile up, demanding a tightrope level of balance.

And truth be told, I found myself spending less time with my older children compared to the younger ones later down the line. Hindsight's a tricky thing, right? Finding balance is a dance. Sometimes you step on a toe or two, but hey, it's all part of the groove. Looking back, I wish I could've orchestrated a more harmonious dance between work and life. Just like any parent, I've had my fair share of challenges: balancing the demands of work and family, navigating the twists and turns of life, and sometimes wishing I had a magical pause button for those moments that slip by too quickly.

Now my heart swells with a mix of pride, gratitude, and a touch of nostalgia, because my kids, the lights of my life, are my inspiration, my endless source of joy. It took time and failure to realize this. Too many years striving to establish my career. Too many years of sacrificing time with my family in order to give my time to my patients. Too long to realize that the healthier and happier I was, the better doctor I could be and the more superior care I could provide. My children's laughter, their unique personalities, have been the bright spots that guide me through the stormy days. They make every hurdle worth the effort expended in the leap.

We're all caught in this whirlwind of ambition, constantly reaching for that next level, that next achievement. The pressure to keep ascending can indeed blur the lines between what we truly need and what we merely want. It's a bit like navigating through fog, isn't it? As they say, regardless of how much you want something, the moment you get it, you want something else.

Take a pause and think about this. We create a never-ending cycle—like mushrooms after rain, new aspirations sprout up, urging us forward. Amid this perpetual juggling act, those quieter, more precious moments can slip through the cracks. The dance, my friends, is a delicate one. We must learn to balance ambition with the simplicity of life's quieter joys, to find a rhythm in the chaos. Here's to navigating the whirlwind and cherishing those moments that make it all worthwhile.

Remember that holding on to the feeling of childlike wonder is like keeping a little piece of magic alive in your heart. It's that ability to marvel at the world, find joy in simple things, and keep the flame of curiosity burning bright. And as far as memories—they do tend to fade with time. But here's the beauty: we have the power to breathe life into them, to keep those cherished moments alive by revisiting them, sharing them, and holding them close.

Other memories need to be cast aside. Carrying the weight of bad memories, regrets, and shame only makes the load heavier. Letting go doesn't mean you don't care; sometimes it means you care enough about your own well-being to release the grip on the past. Some may think it is selfish. I disagree. I call it "conscious self-preservation." Some things are just better left behind. Your history, with all its highs and lows, should never be a crystal ball predicting your destiny. It's a chapter, not the whole story. Embrace the present, creating new memories and shaping a destiny that's uniquely yours.

Here are some insights I have come to see as golden nuggets:

Golden Nuggets

- Change your perspective, and suddenly those failures might not seem as earth shattering. Life's a canvas; paint it with intention.
- Make it a habit to invest in yourself and savor those simple memories.
- Invest in relationships, friends, and family like treasure. These are the bones that hold us upright; with care, these bones flourish.
- When encountering roadblocks, face them head on. When you are stuck, don't withdraw; sometimes the only way out is through.

- Don't try to hit a homer all the time. Life is full of singles and doubles. Appreciate your victories, and they will add up.
- Express yourself. If all your emotions are bottled up, you create a ticking time bomb.
- Realize that resolution always starts from within.
- Embrace imperfections. My mother used to say that the only one who is perfect is God, so since you are not God, it is perfectly okay to try to be better. Life is a journey. Don't expect, at least in this century, to be teleported to another destination without the grind.
- Remember that you are not perfect. You will not be instantly happy. It takes time. Diamonds are a result of millions of years of hardening under pressure.
- Choose joy. The only person who can make you happy is you. You are steering the ship, so choose wisely.
- Pause for a bit, and appreciate the little things.

As we end this list of reminders about savoring life's moments, picture a regular Tuesday. Nothing extraordinary. You're sipping on your favorite cup of coffee, and for a brief moment, everything just clicks. The aroma, the warmth, the simple joy of that perfect sip—it's not a grand adventure, but it feels like winning the day.

Now, let me tell you a little secret: Life's made up of these little victories, these tiny moments. When you add them all up, they make a darn good story. Life is not always about the big milestones, the grand achievements, or the epic adventures. Sometimes it's the quiet joy of a good cup of coffee, unexpected laughter with friends, or a beautiful sunset on an ordinary evening.

So, here's the deal—don't wait for the extraordinary. Embrace the simple pleasures; find delight in the little things. Because when you look back, it's those small, everyday moments that weave the best stories. Life's too short to overlook the magic in the ordinary. Cheers to enjoying the little things—it's where the real story unfolds.

WALKING AWAY

I captured this image in a museum, a stone statue set against the blurred figure of a person walking away in the background. The monochromatic palette emphasizes shades of gray and suggests a world of complexity and subtlety—neither purely light nor purely dark but a blend of both, hence a visual metaphor for life's inherent ambiguities. Just as each shade of gray blends seamlessly into the next, life, too, is full of transitions and nuances, lacking clear-cut lines between right and wrong, past and present, permanence and impermanence.

CHAPTER 7

Shades of Gray: Perspective and Connection

You never really understand a person until you consider things from his point of view ... until you climb inside of his skin and walk around in it.
—HARPER LEE, TO KILL A MOCKINGBIRD

I'm kind of a skills explorer. Every year, I pick a random thing to dive into, making it my low-key New Year's resolution. It's a wild ride, from wrapping my head around quantum physics, to skydiving, to trying my hand at wood carving, or even to mastering a few magic tricks.

I'm all about keeping things interesting and staying mentally nimble. It's like an annual challenge to step out of my comfort zone and soak up new knowledge. The range is all over the place, but that's what keeps life fun and fulfilling. Who knew quantum physics and magic tricks could coexist in the same sentence? This skills exploration is my little tradition to ensure that I'm always learning something new and keeping my brain cells on their toes (though this is physiologically impossible).

Some time ago, I decided to dive into the world of sketching and drawing—a challenge I had long admired from a distance but never thought I could take on. You know, one of those "I'll be a pro in a year" kind of plans. I've been pretty awful at sketching for as long as I can remember. I mean, Leonardo and Michelangelo were Teenage Mutant Ninja Turtles in my teen world, not revered artists. Later, I found myself hooked on drawing just the same.

In my adult life, I started to become increasingly drawn to art and literature. I've been on a bit of a world tour through art museums and galleries, hitting up dozens in various countries and continents. Amsterdam was a highlight, where I hung out with Van Gogh for a bit. Seeing Rembrandt's *Stone Operation* hit me like a sledgehammer—I could feel the pain of the patient and appreciate the apathy from the assistant while totally getting the focus of the healer.

Art has this crazy way of making you feel things, and those moments in front of these masterpieces ... they're like snapshots of shared human experiences, just hanging on a museum wall. Sketching imposes no boundaries, just a devotion to developing infinite possibilities. Using a freehand and willful design gives you full access to imagination. Possibilities exist beyond the box we are so comfortable living in. Art enables us to expand our creative horizons.

Through interpreting art, I learned to find parallels in life. Doing so can offer profound insights and a sense of connection that transcends time, place, and circumstance. This act of drawing comparisons between seemingly disparate experiences helps us make sense of our world and our place within it. It can serve as a source of comfort, inspiration, and understanding, revealing the shared human condition that unites us all. By seeking understanding through similarities in different aspects of life or between historical and contemporary events, we gain a deeper understanding of each.

For instance, leaders studying past conflicts may use historical parallels to navigate modern political crises. This reflection allows them to learn from past mistakes and successes, applying these lessons to current situations. Observing life from another's perspective, we can find parallels and connections with our own experiences, fostering a deeper understanding of the human condition. Finding parallels in life enriches our understanding, connects us with others, and can inspire both personal and collective action. It underscores the recurring themes of human existence and encourages us to learn from the past as we navigate the present and future.

In the midst of this artistic adventure, I stumbled upon some pretty cool connections or parallels between learning to sketch and understanding people better. It's as if the basic principles of drawing have this hidden wisdom that goes beyond the paper and spills into the real world, making connections with folks a bit more profound along the way. Who knew a sketch pad could teach you about life?

Observing life from another's perspective, we can find parallels and connections with our own experiences, fostering a deeper understanding of the human condition.

I probably shouldn't be surprised about this, not just because every aspect of life, every experience we go through, can teach us something but also because this notion that life is a classroom—whether that's biology or art class or any other—was part of my upbringing. Art in its various forms was given equal billing to science and other pursuits by my parents. I wasn't always the best student, but I always loved learning new things, and my parents were great teachers who led by example.

The sketch pad has taught me that I need to see things through a different lens and that I have to adjust my mindset a bit every time I switch between mediums, whether taking a photograph or sketching or painting a canvas. I have shared a bit about where I come from in the belief that in knowing more about me, you are more likely to gain a clearer understanding of how I view the world, including my perhaps unconventional, nuanced views on the nature of success and failure or the spectrum in between the two polarities.

I hope you will see the connection between my life experiences and the person I'm still becoming. If you understand that *connection*, it can assist you in grasping what I mean when I say that life is always full of shades of gray. Nothing is just black and white in life.

The Principles of Sketching

As I just mentioned, I've tried my hand at photography, something that you've already encountered through the images that start every chapter. I've dabbled in painting, metalwork, and sculpture. I have dozens of projects—some pure art, some artistic practicalities—in various stages around my house and studio and dozens upon dozens more in my head. But a lot of these interests share aspects of sketching.

Even as a rank amateur who started with more doodling (and a whole lot of erasing) than sketching, it didn't take long to figure out that sketching had its holy trinity of fundamentals, three things that I had to crack to unlock the secrets of this art form, even if it's been quite the ride figuring out those keys.

The Holy Trinity of Sketching

1. **Composition**
2. **Perspective (light, visual depth, and background)**
3. **Shading**

As I delve deeper into the realm of sketching, I've come to realize that it serves as a metaphor, imparting lessons on grasping perspective. The art of sketching draws parallels with honing emotional insight in understanding people. This heightened awareness fosters a relational understanding essential for both personal and business acumen. It's undeniable that every facet of our actions is interconnected and relational.

Let's play out this analogy and start with the fundamentals of sketching—composition. You can literally draw anything in the universe using a few geometrical shapes: squares, rectangles, triangles, and circles. Think of the human face, which is essentially an oval, one that contains circular eyes and mouth, a triangle nose, all balanced on a centerline and symmetrical, and another triangle formed from the outside of the eyes to the chin. A master composition is about achieving balance in such features and in how they are made to appear three-dimensional. That's where this shading business comes in. Abstract lines create flat and two-dimensional images; these shades of gray construct a three-dimensional image that is closer to life. Too much shading ruins your composition, turning everything dark, just like too much salt can ruin a meal.

Similar to these four basic geometrical shapes, people fall into four different personality types, as defined in an article that first appeared in the journal *Nature Human Behavior*,[9] an approach that applies hordes of data and that moves beyond the magazine-style self-help versions of personality type and traits with which most of us are aware:

Four Personality Types

Average: High in neuroticism and extraversion while low in openness.

Reserved: Emotionally stable but not open or neurotic. They are not particularly extroverted but are somewhat agreeable and conscientious.

Role Model: Low in neuroticism and high in all the other traits. The likelihood that someone is a role model increases dramatically with age. Average in openness.

Self-Centered: Very high in extroversion and below average in openness, agreeableness, and conscientiousness. The likelihood that someone is self-centered also increases dramatically with age.

There is a key difference between personality traits and types. Traits are fluid and exist on a continuum, while types are rigid and categorical. Traits allow for a nuanced combination of characteristics, whereas types simplify individuals into defined groups. There are five key traits—agreeableness, openness, extroversion, neuroticism, and conscientiousness—applied in this study that basically shape how

9 Martin Gerlach, Beatrice Farb, Willian Reville, and Luís A. Nunes Amaral, "A Robust Data-Driven Approach Identifies Four Personality Types across Four Large Data Sets," *Nature Human Behaviour* 2 (2018): 735–742, https://doi.org/10.1038/s41562-018-0419-z.

people tick.[10] (Neuroticism as a personality trait is characterized by emotional instability, irritability, anxiety, self-doubt, depression, and other negative feelings.[11]) Once you wrap your head around these traits and the basic personality types they create, it's like having a cheat code to understanding people better. It's a game changer in navigating the intricate dance of human interactions.

Composition

With sketching, you start with small strokes. Each shape, from the simplest circle, begins with tiny, deliberate strokes. Slowly, you build on them, extending and expanding until they seamlessly connect, giving rise to the complete and desired form. It's a process in which every detail, every curve, is meticulously crafted from those initial small strokes. The art lies in the gradual expansion of these strokes, a patient journey of creation where the envisioned shape gradually takes form, stroke by stroke.

Connecting with people, much like the delicate process of sketching, follows a similar rhythm. When you meet someone new, it's easy to succumb to the temptation of firing off a rapid succession of questions, hoping to unveil the entire picture in one go. However, just as in sketching, you start with fine strokes using the finest HB pencils; this approach might reveal only a fraction of the intricate puzzle. Instead, consider the art of relying on cues and subtleties rather than bombarding them with relentless inquiries. It's akin to initiating with a bit of small talk and actively listening, allowing people to gradually open up.

10 Ibid.

11 Ibid.

In doing so, you uncover answers to questions you may have never explicitly asked. It's the slow unveiling, stroke by stroke, that allows the full and rich picture of a person to emerge, creating a connection that goes beyond the surface. We can utilize diverse tools such as body language and nonverbal cues and learn techniques like making eye contact without intense staring, leaning forward to express interest, and nodding to signify agreement. Maintaining a comfortable distance strikes a balance. When executed thoughtfully, these methods not only enhance communication but mirror the gradual commitment seen in the art of sketching.

Sketching is a series of clarifying steps. Like most things in life, you move from rough first steps to more defined commitments. Throw down that bold outline without the groundwork of a rough sketch, and you might end up with a messy definition disaster. Erasing the first soft pencil strokes is manageable, but eradicating mistakes in that bold outline is like dealing with chaos—messy as hell. Harsh lines? They can be downright unpleasant and irritating. So can first interactions with new people. And if we only go with first impressions, we may misjudge the person entirely, just as they might with us.

We have all experienced this, probably more often than we care to remember. For me, as a brown-skinned man with an accent, occasionally being judged by others on surfaces and assumptions—on rough, incomplete sketches, if you will—happens all the time. This means that I always have to work a little harder to prove myself. But I also have to be careful and become reactive, which means being purposeful so that I don't make first judgments reciprocal.

Let me share a few stories about different personality types and the strategies you can use to navigate situations effectively while staying focused on achieving your goals.

THE ONE-UPPER

Years ago, I met a man who turned every conversation into a contest. Let's call him Peter. Peter wasn't just competitive; he thrived on being the biggest, the best, and the most impressive in the room. Within five minutes of meeting him, I noticed the pattern.

If I mentioned an accomplishment, he'd top it. "I've worked with two hundred clinicians in my group," I said casually.

Peter leaned back in his chair and smirked. "Oh, two hundred? I used to manage five hundred. Back in my prime, I had entire hospitals under my leadership."

I decided to pivot. "Quality over quantity, though," I countered with a smile. "My team delivers top-notch results."

Peter immediately jumped in. "Quality? Let me tell you—when I was in charge, no one could touch the kind of results we delivered."

It dawned on me then: This wasn't a discussion. It was a performance. Peter's need to feel superior meant no amount of logic, proof, or argument would ever convince him otherwise. If I kept trying to "win," I'd only frustrate myself and derail the purpose of our meeting.

So I shifted gears. I nodded along and occasionally complimented his achievements. "That's impressive," I said. "You've really done a lot."

With his ego stroked, Peter became more agreeable. I quickly guided the conversation back to the reason I was there. Without much resistance, Peter agreed to my proposal, and I left with everything I needed.

Sometimes, winning isn't about proving a point. When you recognize someone's need to dominate, let them feel like the star of the show. Adjust your approach, and you'll get what you came for without unnecessary conflict.

THE ETERNAL COMPLAINER

Then there was Lori. Lori wasn't competitive—she was chronically dissatisfied. Every suggestion, idea, or solution was met with a complaint.

"I think we should try this new approach," I suggested during a team meeting.

Lori sighed. "That'll never work. It's too complicated."

I offered an alternative. "What if we streamlined the process this way?"

Another sigh. "We've tried that before. It's useless."

At first, I felt frustrated. Her negativity felt like a wall I couldn't get around. But then I realized that Lori wasn't rejecting the ideas themselves—she just needed to feel heard. Complaining was her way of asserting control over the situation.

Instead of pushing back, I leaned into her mindset. "You're absolutely right," I said. "There are definitely challenges with this idea. What do you think we could do differently?"

Lori paused, caught off guard. She hesitated and then offered a small suggestion. I built on it. "That's a great point. Let's refine it further together." Gradually, she became less defensive and more collaborative.

By the end of the meeting, we'd come up with a workable plan, and Lori felt ownership over the solution. The key was not fighting her complaints but redirecting them into contributions.

When dealing with complainers, don't shut them down. Acknowledge their concerns and gently guide them toward constructive input. You'll turn their negativity into something useful.

Understanding people is the key to navigating any interaction. Whether you're dealing with a one-upper, a complainer, an indecisive individual, or a skeptic, the solution lies in recognizing their personality and adapting your approach. It's not about changing who you are—it's about meeting people where they are to achieve the outcome you want. When you master this skill, no personality is too challenging to work with.

We also should always try to understand the state of mind of the person we are dealing with. Think about how your own personality changes when you have a serious headache. Aren't you more likely to have a short fuse? The same might be said for the customer who has been notified of a delay, the person across a desk during tough negotiations, the job candidate nervous about an interview. We're not always seeing the whole person, let alone the person at their best, so we are not able to understand their perspective.

The same goes for our patients in hospitals. Some are just more difficult to manage. It's a whole new ball game and an additional complexity when you add in unfamiliar places, cultures, and backgrounds. I couldn't fully know what my patients are experiencing at that moment any more than I might know if they had past negative experiences with other doctors or other hospitals. I couldn't know their shades of gray. At times I am just a moment in their timelines and am exposed to only one of their dimensions.

I try to see the good in others. Let's face it, though—that's not always easy. Just as I sometimes get down on myself, I'm human like anyone and sometimes am too quick to cast judgment. I must say, however, that central among the lessons in my life is that doing so is dangerous and harms the self just as much as the person you are judging, and as a result, I have learned to remind myself that all of us have unique experiences and all of us might be very different people on any given day.

The majority of people and patients are easy to deal with. When they are not, I try to remember that I am not defined by their version of me. On the other hand, when I have shown restraint and probed deeper into their perspective in situations like these, people calm down, and a handful of them even offer sincere apologies. Sometimes those acts of contrition don't come until the next day or even weeks or months later, but I appreciate it when they do arrive. The harder part, of course, is learning to let go of the negative feelings toward those who never admit when they are wrong. The only thing we can control is making certain we don't behave in similar ways—flying off the handle because of our own grievances or insecurities—whether with strangers, coworkers, friends, or family.

Over time, I've learned the importance of checking the "basement" of my brain, the medulla oblongata. This area governs our instinctual responses when threatened—freeze, fight, or flee. By taking a few seconds to recognize when we're operating from this "basement," our reactions can become more measured and controlled. I've realized that regardless of who is at fault, losing patience and reacting impulsively often means facing the consequences ourselves.

Let's talk beyond encounters with strangers and tackle the even trickier terrain of relationships and friendships. Those babies need time, a serious commitment, and some good old hard work. It's an investment, you know, potentially the most valuable one you'll make. Building a real connection with people? That takes patience, being present, showing empathy, keeping it real with honesty and transparency, and throwing in some good old vulnerability.

It's an investment, yeah, but give it time, and you might end up with a friendship that lasts, a companionship that rocks, and, most importantly, trust that's unshakeable. So, just like you wouldn't start drawing with a bold line, maybe hold off on getting too familiar too soon in your connections. It's all about laying the foundation before you go all in. On the contrary, be prepared that you may have gotten it wrong from the start, and it's okay to be wrong about your early relationships with people. If it's not working, maybe it's not meant to be. Don't let this ruin your future relationships. Always be ready to start again. And it all starts with trying to understand their personality traits and figuring out where they fit in.

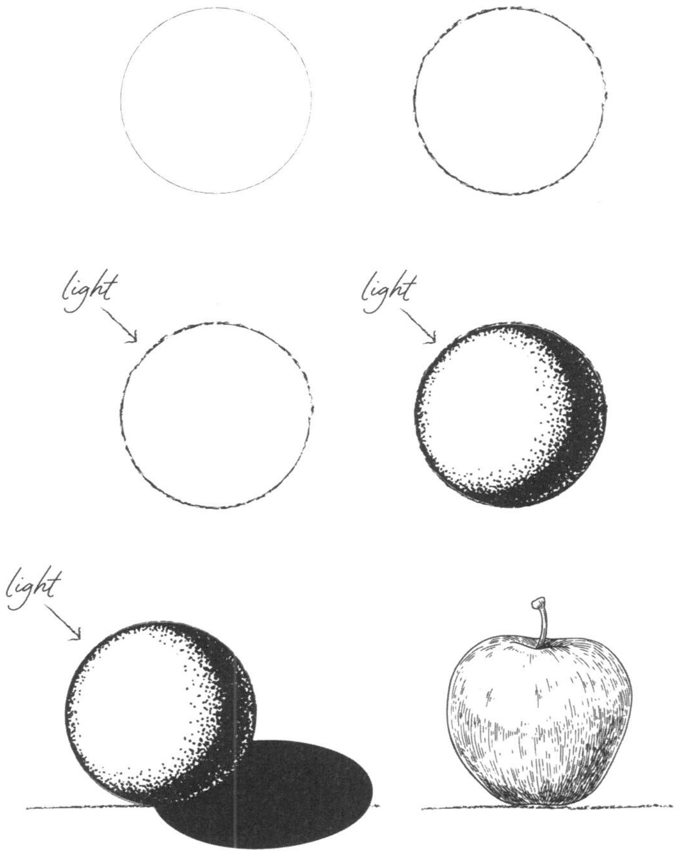

Perspective

Perspective, the second principle of sketching, is like that "let's put things into perspective" moment. Light is the ultimate perspective for drawing. It's all about the relativity of an object with its surroundings. Think about it—without perspective, you're stuck with a two-dimensional, dull, impersonal, and lifeless object.

Imagine yourself standing on a bridge above a busy highway, all those folks zipping by in their cars. To us, they're just "passengers." We don't know squat about them—no clue if they're fathers, mothers, friends. We don't know their backgrounds. We have no clue what they're going through. We're kind of stuck in that place. All we see are these basic geometrical shapes, not the rich tapestry of their lives. It's a reminder that without perspective, everything is a bit flat and one-dimensional.

When drawing, your perspective comes from light. Light illuminates but also creates shadows. Light and visual depth make the image hop, jump, and dance off the canvas, and this provides shape and perspective. It brings life to an object and transforms it from a two-dimensional object into a three-dimensional structure. In order to get a natural look, the object needs to emerge out of the shadows. Your object has to bask in an understanding of where the illumination is coming from. It's like the origins of a story—knowing where the light falls and where the shadows dance. To me, light in sketching is like understanding where people are coming from—their life philosophies, relationships, interests, hobbies, careers, habits, experiences, and life scenarios. It's delving into their past to define their present.

And as you navigate this journey, you might just stumble upon similarities. This self-discovery can be a compass, guiding you to rewrite your own story. Similar to visual depth in sketching, understanding people's backgrounds is the key to forging deeper connections. You've heard the

To me, light in sketching is like understanding where people are coming from—their life philosophies, relationships, interests, hobbies, careers, habits, experiences, and life scenarios. It's delving into their past to define their present.

saying "Know your audience"? Well, knowing their background helps you find those common threads, creating a sense of familiarity. And let's face it—everyone is more comfortable with the familiar. I'm always intrigued by people who share similar hobbies or have been to the same places I have visited. It's like finding your tribe. Doing your research, just like in sketching, adds that layer of depth that turns a casual connection into something more profound. Sometimes life gives you a jolt and your perspectives are challenged. As you read about some important parts of my personal story, you ran into experiences that tested me—including moments when I wasn't up to the test. If I'd have stopped there, I wouldn't have a story to tell at all. One of the biggest lessons of my life has been learning how to change perspective, which is all about learning to grow from experiences.

I carry very real scars from when I was abused as a kid and from the bullies who tortured me in medical school, but the wounds they inflicted on me are nothing compared to the drive to change what I was capable of changing when I saw the despair of that little boy whose mother died because I could not get her the medicine she needed after thugs burned our storeroom.

Without that boy's loss, I might never have reached a place in my life where I could, decades later, start the Pioneer Medical Foundation. Had I never cleaned carpets for a living, I might not have the ability to connect with people at all levels and recognize how each of us has our own struggles. Had my need to obtain a green card and practice medicine in a country I have come to love not offered a vulnerability that an unscrupulous healthcare company used to their advantage, I might never have discovered the drive to learn the ins and outs of business and start my own. Perspective is a powerful thing.

Shading

Now, shading, the third pillar of sketching, is like magic. Shading with different spectrums of white and black is what adds that sense of depth, realism, and dimension to the canvas. It's the art of blending colors, and that introduces an emotional tone, creating a vibe that speaks to us. When you're sketching, nothing is truly black and white. You need those shades of gray to fully appreciate the depth and expanse of an object, just as we must make emotional connections with people. It's what takes your sketch from a flat image to a masterpiece that tells a nuanced story.

Real people are full of shades of gray. Rarely can someone be neatly categorized as purely good or bad. You've seen that learning a bit about others allows us to see them as fellow humans and, at the same time, as fallible. Parents aren't perfect, family is not perfect, friends aren't perfect, workers aren't flawless, and bosses aren't infallible. We all come with our unique mix of strengths and weaknesses, successes and failures.

Understanding this has given me the ability to better comprehend that no one is perfect. People can be imperfectly perfect, and they can still be accepted and appreciated. If you set your bar too high, expecting perfection, you might find yourself alone and miserable. Embracing the shades of gray in people allows for richer, more meaningful connections, acknowledging the beauty in imperfection. It's what makes us wonderfully human.

I love to sketch, but I don't regard it as a strength. I'm still learning. I'd argue that when it comes to people, we're all still learning. There's a lot about people that I didn't begin to understand until middle age after undergoing personal failures, including relationship failures. Life is a continuous journey. We are always evolving.

At a different stage in my life, my focus was more on getting what I wanted rather than delving into the needs and perspectives of others. Understanding people is an intricate journey. We are all guilty of making assumptions. We all wear our uniforms.

When I lived in Chicago, every morning when I commuted to my job as a researcher, I wore a coat and tie. I'd finish my day, return home, rest a bit, eat, and then change into the coveralls I wore for my night work as a carpet cleaner. Back onto the subway I went. I was clearly the same person, yet you wouldn't have known it by the way I was treated by strangers on my commute. People reacted entirely differently to me in one "uniform" than they did in the other. We all have a tendency to make assumptions about others without delving into their unique experiences and perspectives. This oversight can lead to misunderstandings and missed connections.

Another shortfall in understanding people often stems from the inclination to judge based on surface-level attributes. Overlooking the depth of individual stories and backgrounds can result in biased opinions and hinder the development of empathy—not to be confused with pity or sympathy. To better understand people, it's essential to embrace open-mindedness and curiosity. Actively listen, ask thoughtful questions, and seek to comprehend diverse viewpoints. Recognize the uniqueness of each person's narrative, and cultivate empathy to bridge the gaps that may arise from our failures in understanding.

Through continuous self-reflection and a commitment to learning, we can navigate the complexities of human connection more effectively. The joy in life, the joy that fills us with emotion and vibrancy, is found in blending shades and colors. Stick to one dimension, and we never make meaningful connections, and those connections will always be more important than how we earn our living or how much money we make. I have met fellow carpet cleaners who were every bit as rich in the meaningful connections they have cemented among friends and family as the healthcare professionals with whom I work today. Where do such connections start? By not just focusing on what you want or how you see the world. Self-centeredness only makes for a lopsided drawing.

Take a risk. Pick up a pencil. It's all erasable. Draw who you are, what you see. Study others, but don't try to blindly emulate them. It's entirely your choice if you ever share your attempts with others. When you're ready, try something difficult but close to home—a human face. You may or may not feel you ever do your subject justice, but I guarantee you will see that face in a way you never have before.

That's the funny thing about attempting to master composition, perspective, and shading. You will see beyond the shape of a nose or the fine wrinkle lines at the eyes that accompany a smile; you'll glimpse something of the personality contained within that person beyond the face, want to learn about their experiences, ponder what has shaped how they have come to view the world. Approach the people you meet with the same openness, the same close study, the same attentiveness; appreciate all that makes them unique, and you will have taken a first step toward making meaningful connections.

That is the anatomy of understanding people, finding parallels in life. Sketching and life—both a bit messy, a bit complex, but full of observations that can make things a whole lot more interesting.

STILL IN THE SHELL

A crab emerges from its burrow, as if hesitantly stepping into the world outside. With a vibrant blue shell, bold red legs, and a large white claw held aloft, the crab stands out against the muted, earthy tones of the surrounding mud. The contrast between its bright colors and the subdued environment symbolizes a moment of transformation—of leaving behind the comfort of its "shell" to face what lies beyond and embracing the challenges of that world.

CHAPTER 8

When a Box Is Not a Box: The Power of Creative Thinking

You can't use up creativity. The more you use, the more you have.
—MAYA ANGELOU

There are a lot of clichés when it comes to creative thinking:

"Color outside the lines."

"Break the mold."

"Play by your own rules."

"Think outside the box."

It's not bad advice. But it doesn't go far enough for me. I'd rather ask, "What if there are no lines, no mold, no rules? What if there is no box?"

Think about that for a minute. Rather than simply asking ourselves for original outside-the-box thinking, what if we deconstructed the whole thought process? Rather than just challenging conventional thinking, what if we applied entirely new methods of insight or took something that works as a solution elsewhere and modified it to work in another environment, which is honestly where most invention comes from? Why not create your own box?

Creative thinking is the art of seeing the world not as it is, but as it could be. It's the spark that ignites new ideas, the courage to break from the familiar, and the curiosity to explore possibilities that others might overlook. Creative thinking is about connecting dots that don't seem to connect, embracing the unexpected, and turning problems into opportunities for something entirely original. It's the mindset that says, "What if?" and isn't afraid of where the answer might lead.

Creative thinking is about connecting dots that don't seem to connect, embracing the unexpected, and turning problems into opportunities for something entirely original.

You've probably read enough by now to recognize how much I value the concept of "thinking differently," but I do so in ways that create value. I often say, "Let's think about this differently, but not like a circus clown." I mean no offense to circus clowns, but some people misinterpret distinctive, original thinking not by valuing the substance of ideas but rather by their audacity or shock value. Shock has value, but not for long. And believe me, when you've seen as many patients and attended thousands of corporate meetings as I have, I'm pretty immune to shock.

We need original thinking that can move us closer to our objectives or mission. Accomplishing clear objectives often means that great ideas come from unexpected people. If, that is, we're smart enough to recognize them. That's a whole different reason for recognizing and respecting everyone around us. You never know where the solution to a problem may come from. A lot of the time, we can't even identify the source of the problem.

Consider this example. Hedy Lamarr, too often admired only for her beauty and her presence as a 1930s and 1940s film star, was also an inventor and is today credited for being the "grandmother" of Wi-Fi, GPS, and Bluetooth technology. This stems from her partnership with George Antheil on their patented invention of "frequency hopping" radio waves (now known as frequency-hopping spread spectrum technology) meant to conceal the guidance systems of Allied torpedoes.

An immigrant to America from Austria in 1937, she was raised in a Jewish family and likely lost many friends and family members to the Holocaust and often used her fame to support American war efforts. Lamarr was particularly alarmed at how mercilessly German U-boats were sinking Allied warships and commercial ships. Their invention, inspired by the concept of the player piano, ensured that by moving a signal swiftly across the possible frequency bandwidth, US long-range torpedo signals would never linger long enough to be intercepted.

While most laughed at the notion of a Hollywood beauty being an inventor, and while the patent for frequency hopping remained unused until after its expiration, the critical idea behind her invention has been central to the digital age, with applications she could never have foreseen. Her story is not at all unusual. Encouraged by her engineer father, she had tinkered with inventions most of her life and had tools and worktables set up in her on-location film-studio trailers.

Like most creative thinkers, she not only removed limits from how she approached potential inventions; she was guided by practical applications and problem solving (she also invented an improved traffic signal and a tablet similar to modern carbonated beverages). Lamarr is just one example among tens of thousands. Nearly every major invention has an improbable story behind it or an unexpected inventor.

My own style of thinking is usually the kind that gets me in trouble—remember the vegetable-cutting episode that got me fired on my first day on the job when my new boss accused me of being something similar to a circus clown? In my defense, by nature I was intrigued by processes, hence my desire to identify the most efficient way to slice vegetables. This way of thinking is part of what drove me to push harder and explore beyond medicine, whether in art, writing, or process acceleration. I remain unapologetically curious.

While reducing a patient to a set of biological imperatives is antithetical to my belief about healing, the reality is that the human body is a mesmerizingly beautiful, intricately complex, interdependent, living machine. This may sound odd, but as a physician, I love treating critically ill patients. It's not that I take pleasure in their suffering; rather, I feel most capable when I can make the greatest impact for those in need. With difficult cases, I know that I can practice my art better. I take pride in being the one who always tried to see the patient first. I love that I can be of help, including in the process of finding the elusive diagnosis. And, of course, who could not love being part of the team who helps a very sick patient get better? That's all part of the terrifyingly beautiful world of practicing medicine.

But it's also true that we treat human bodies inside created environments like hospitals and that our ability to treat patients is often determined in large part by nonbiological realities such as what insurance will pay for, what makes a hospital remain profitable, how medical groups survive, what is possible within the limits of technological and human resources, and what processes are required to make those resources viable. As a result, I am intrigued by processes and logistics and their role in achieving positive health outcomes as I contribute to healing a body or a process to help thousands.

From my earliest days as a hospitalist, I was constantly aware of how often healthcare has created inefficient, sometimes even perilous processes. Some of the complicated logistics involved with how hospitals and medical groups care for patients are rooted in the scale of what they do and in the inherent bureaucracy that comes with any sizable institution. Some of those complications originate in the simple audacity and sheer responsibility of what is involved in trying to treat injury and disease.

Then there are the amazing (and very expensive) toys at our disposal, ones we feel we had better use if we are to justify their cost. It was in this early period of personal and professional turmoil and amid an overwhelming workload that I began to ponder if there were more efficient ways of doing a lot of fairly ordinary, albeit important, things around day-to-day hospital medicine.

Eventually that sort of thinking led me to curiosity about the Toyota Production System (TPS). TPS has become recognized throughout manufacturing worldwide and has completely upended how much of production works. In the car-manufacturing universe, the objective of TPS is to eliminate waste and shorten lead times to deliver high-quality vehicles. The basic philosophy of TPS is based on two pillars.[12]

The first concept of TPS in Japanese is *jidoka*—which can be loosely translated as "automation with a human touch"—based on the concepts of stopping immediately when abnormalities are detected to prevent defective products from being produced and improving

---

12 Athira Krishna and Dr. Sini V Nair, "Toyota Production System as a Benchmark to Improve Business Productivity," *International Journal of Innovative Science and Research Technology* 3, no. 1 (January 2018), https://ijisrt.com/wp-content/uploads/2018/01/Toyota-Production-System-As-A-Benchmark-To-Improve-Business-Productivity.pdf.

productivity to eliminate the need for people to be simply watching over machines.[13]

The second pillar is *just in time*, based on the concept of synchronizing production processes—linking all plants and their production processes in a continuous flow—by making only what is needed, when it is needed, and in the amount needed. TPS has become so ubiquitous in manufacturing that we have all learned the downside of the just-in-time concept by way of the disrupted supply chains we experienced during the COVID-19 pandemic.[14]

Remember the toilet paper shortage? The lack of face masks? The run on sriracha? But that's manufacturing, right? What on earth does TPS have to do with healthcare?

I became so fascinated with the potential applications of TPS that in 2007 I enrolled in a TPS course and found myself in the unfamiliar environs of a Toyota plant in Japan working alongside autoworkers. I might be a long way distant from the inventors who took Hedy Lamarr's ideas and applied them to wireless communications, but I couldn't help but wonder if there were TPS applications that could improve patient outcomes. The presence of such a rough idea didn't help the imposter syndrome I suffered wondering if I could really do what would be asked of me.

You can imagine how I felt in Japan alongside autoworkers and engineers. A harsh reality check happened on the first day on the job at the Toyota plant in Fukuoka. The Toyota Motor Kyushu, Inc. facility is located in the Miyata area of Fukuoka Prefecture. This plant is responsible for manufacturing several Toyota and Lexus models. I certainly did not expect that my first "educational" experience was being placed in front of an air conditioner assembly line and given a

13 Ibid.

14 Ibid.

task to decrease the time to assemble the air conditioner unit inside the cars. It felt more like a plot from a comedy movie than my reality.

Despite joining other participants who worked in healthcare, none of whom had engineering backgrounds, we were all a little unhinged. I had been expecting to be placed in a biomedical scenario, not on a line making air conditioners! But I thought, *Oh well, what do I have to lose?* That's a classic example of an "open space."

No one expected much from us to begin with, so in the absence of expectation I thought, *This is the time to absorb it all.* I watched the assembly belt, thought about the cars and the humongous robots, and began to break things down—kind of like organizing vegetables to be cut.

I observed the flow of the long belt and the sequence in which it delivered supplies, noting that the assembly table was arranged in a U shape. This prompted me to consider how to minimize unnecessary movement, a key principle in lean methodology. My first thought was to reduce the distance employees had to walk to access supplies. That would not only improve efficiency but also decrease the likelihood of parts being dropped or damaged. Such thinking—simple adjustments, like streamlining workflows and eliminating wasted motion—aligns perfectly with TPS's emphasis on reducing waste and enhancing productivity. What I began recognizing was something about logistics and the relationship between people and space, about how the design of a room could enhance those logistics. In short, TPS thinking. Fun fact about the Toyota company: long before it got into the car business, Toyota began in 1926 as Toyota Automatic Loom Works—it was a textile company. I firmly believe that their innovative approach and outside-the-box thinking finally led to their first Toyota Model AA in 1936.

Even in that foreign environment, I began thinking about how I might put such ideas to work once I returned home. I knew right away the problem I wanted to tackle—sepsis. My instincts had always told me that this dire medical problem requires a certain clinical attention almost as much as a logistical one: The Surviving Sepsis Campaign implementation was the perfect answer.

Sepsis is a life-threatening medical emergency that occurs when the body's immune system has an extreme response to an infection. Sepsis can lead to organ dysfunction, shock, multiple organ failure, and death. Essentially, the infection-fighting processes turn on the body, going into a kind of hyperdrive, causing the organs to work poorly (think of an assembly-line belt sped up a thousandfold). The most important weapon in fighting the effects of sepsis is early treatment, which is precisely why treating sepsis is as much a logistics issue as a medical one.

Sepsis is the sixth-most-common reason for hospitalization in the United States. For patients presenting with severe sepsis, mortality rates are approximately 30 percent, and sepsis remains the most expensive reason for hospitalization.[15] When organ failure sets in, sepsis has a mortality rate of around 42 percent, which is comparable to a heart attack.[16] But if you treat sepsis within three hours and with corrective therapy like IV fluids, antibiotics on board, etc., you decrease the mortality to about 18 percent.[17]

---

15 D. C. Angus, W. T. Linde-Zwirble, J. Lidicker, G. Clermont, J. Carcillo, and M. R. Pinsky, "Epidemiology of Severe Sepsis in the United States: Analysis of Incidence, Outcome, and Associated Costs of Care," *Critical Care Medicine* 29, no. 7 (July 2001): 1303–1310.

16 M. M. Levy, L. E. Evans, and A. M. Rhodes, "The Surviving Sepsis Campaign Bundle: 2018 Update," *Intensive Care Medicine* 44, no. 6 (2018): 925–928.

17 "AHRQ Report to Congress Describes Sepsis' Burgeoning Burden on Hospital Care," Agency for Healthcare Research and Quality, September 2024, https://www.ahrq.gov/news/sepsis-report.html.

I proposed a lead project focused on the emergency department (ED), as the majority of sepsis diagnoses originate there. I immediately began picturing the "spaghetti maps" I had been taught in the TPS course. A spaghetti map (or diagram) is a visual representation using a continuous flow line tracing the path of an item or activity through a process, like how the parts of an air-conditioning unit move through the assembly line from first step to completion. They enable you to identify redundancies in the workflow and opportunities to expedite process flow.

I observed that sometimes patients were removed from triage and told to wait in the main ED holding area. Busy periods with lots of other emergencies pushed them down the treatment list and caused further delays. Every delay risked worsening their condition and accelerated damage to their organs. The key to treating sepsis is to rapidly identify it and immediately provide the patient with the right therapy.

Ironically, the initial criteria for identifying sepsis are the simplest measurements that don't require a physician to ascertain—pulse, heart rate, temperature, respiratory rate. Then you move on to associated findings of confusion or signs of kidney failure or liver failure. If two out of four primary criteria are elevated, you order labs to screen for sepsis, so the faster you can screen a patient, the faster you can start the treatment.

Based on our initial findings from the project, we implemented changes in ED protocols in order to cut any wait periods, including developing a new patient questionnaire and taking patient vitals first. If they were elevated in two categories, then their route was changed completely so that they bypassed triage and went directly into the ED for treatment. We also created new sepsis orders that ensure all measures required for treatment are in a bundle and not overlooked by any ordering provider. These measures ensure that critical components like hydration, antibiotics, etc. are administered within an optimal time frame and significantly improve outcomes.

We implemented these new protocols in 2009. Prior to their implementation, in our hospital system sepsis patients who had organ failure had a mortality rate of about 38 percent. After implementation, that number fell to less than 12 percent. Keep in mind that in medicine, saving a single life is powerful. It is an experience most will never have, and it never leaves you. To make simple alterations in a system and save thousands upon thousands of lives seems most gratifying.

It is true that I applied some of the efficiency and quality standards that are part of TPS to help jump start this turnaround, but that's nothing more than the mechanism that originated the idea. The real point is that I had to think differently. I had to stop thinking just like a doctor and look beyond to find a solution, and the same is true to approach any problems that come our way, in order to see the application of the TPS pattern of approach.

During my time in Japan, the constant question asked of me was "Man, what are you doing here?" I usually offered some funny answer like "I got lost on my way to the hospital," but the reality was that I was there for exactly the reasons I understood later in life—to break out of any boxes my formal training, my culture, and my personality had placed me in.

We each have our own eccentricities. We each love different curiosities. We have individual fixations. You might own fifteen different surfboards or fifty fishing rods or a thousand vinyl albums. You might like realism; I might like abstract art. We've read different books. We like different movies. We all have habits, good and bad. But all those things that make up parts of who we are can become prisons that restrict our imagination *or* they can become conduits to enhance creativity.

At the end of the day, the walls that form the boxes around our thinking are of our own making. That means they are ours to destroy as well. And it means that we can choose to make new boxes or, if we dare, think in dimensions where boxes cannot exist.

On a different note, the Toyota Production System emphasizes continuous improvement (*kaizen*) and respect for people. These principles encourage experimentation and view failures as opportunities for learning and growth. The idea positions innovation as a journey rather than a destination—a process inherently filled with missteps and recalibrations.

When projects become "extremely complicated beyond human comprehension," they often fail because traditional methods and rigid thinking can no longer keep pace. This is where TPS principles shine; by breaking down complexity into manageable parts, encouraging collaboration, and fostering a culture where failure is not stigmatized but analyzed and understood, innovation can thrive.

The process of *hansei* (Japanese for "reflective thinking") in TPS—where teams analyze what went wrong and how to improve—mirrors the theme of learning from failure.[18] It's not about avoiding mistakes but about building resilience and adaptability through them.

True innovation requires a paradigm shift in how we perceive failure—not as a setback but as an integral part of the creative process. By connecting the structured approach of TPS with a mindset open to exploring and embracing failure, you create a powerful narrative about overcoming obstacles and achieving growth in even the most complex, seemingly insurmountable situations.

For much of human history, we celebrated individuals who saw the world as a vast, interconnected system, encouraging curiosity

---

18 Jona Tarlengco, "Hansei: A Self-Reflection and Continuous Improvement Lean System," Safety Culture, February 13, 2024, https://safetyculture.com/topics/hansei/.

across disciplines. Yet in the last few centuries, we've been taught to narrow our focus, to specialize in a single field and master that alone—like peering through a keyhole instead of opening the door to see the full picture. But history's greatest innovators defied that constraint. Benjamin Franklin wasn't just a politician; he studied tides, revolutionized mail systems, and contributed to science. Leonardo da Vinci wasn't just a painter; he was a mathematician, philosopher, sculptor, and engineer who designed war machines centuries ahead of his time. Even Steve Jobs wasn't limited to software development—his genius lay in blending design, simplicity, and branding into a vision that reshaped entire industries. The lesson here is clear: don't let specialization confine you. Instead, seek to understand the broader paradigm, explore connections across fields, and allow curiosity to guide you toward seeing the bigger picture. True innovation lies in looking beyond what you know.

In the end, I'll leave you with this: Practice thinking differently, and embrace creative approaches. Consider how another expert might approach the same challenge. For me, "thinking differently" is a guiding principle—one that often demands breaking down the idols we hold dear to spark real change. You may be surprised at how many revered ideas must be reimagined to create something new.

CONNECTIONS

This striking image shows a herd of elephants walking together through an African savanna under the shadow of a grand baobab tree. The baobab tree, ancient and expansive, stands as a symbol of endurance and wisdom, much like the elephants moving beneath it. Elephants are known for their deep emotional bonds and complex social structures, often demonstrating empathy, cooperation, and protective instincts toward one another. They mourn their dead, care for their young collectively, and rely on the wisdom of elder members, especially matriarchs, to lead them through challenges, much like the way emotional intelligence fosters connection, resilience, and guidance in human communities.

CHAPTER 9

The Elephant Rider: Leveraging Emotional Intelligence

It is very important to understand that emotional intelligence is not the opposite of intelligence, it is not the triumph of heart over head–it is the unique intersection of both.

—DAVID CARUSO

In his 2006 book, *The Happiness Hypothesis: Finding Modern Truth in Ancient Wisdom*, social psychologist Jonathan Haidt uses the metaphor of an elephant and its rider when introducing the concept of emotional intelligence quotient, or EQ.[19] In this image, the emotional side of human personality is represented by the elephant, and the rational brain (IQ) is the rider perched atop the six-ton behemoth. The rider holds the reins. The rider appears to be the leader, the one in control. But the rider's control is precarious because the rider is so small relative to the elephant.

19 Jonathan Haidt, *The Happiness Hypothesis: Finding Modern Truth in Ancient Wisdom* (Basic Books, 2006).

Anytime the elephant and the rider disagree about which direction to go, the rider, completely overmatched, is going to lose. Do you doubt this? Just drop the six-ton elephant and picture instead a six-year-old human and tell me you don't believe emotions exert dominance. Or for that matter, step back and take a look at yourself the next time you're in an argument with your partner. Folks, I am married to a lovely Latina, so I had no choice but to learn this skill.

For better or for worse, all of us interact with the world with a mix of IQ and EQ. We really *want* to believe that IQ rules the day. This is particularly true in the workplace. The "want to" portion, I mean. The presence of emotion, even if it is just simmering under the surface (or behind the boss's back) is as present at work as it is on the home front. We ignore the power of emotion at our peril.

If we want to be successful when working and living with others, we have to amp up our EQ. We take courses and do exercises and expand our knowledge to improve our IQ, right? (Or at least that's what you tell yourself when you do that morning puzzle or look up something on YouTube—I see you.) Why do we dismiss the importance of improving our EQ?

In the medical field, the importance of EQ is front and center. Or at least its absence is. We've all encountered medical professionals who might be quite brilliant but whose "bedside manner" leaves something to be desired. There are few professions where the stakes feel higher. One night during my residency, I learned a lesson that shaped every patient interaction I've had since. I remember seeing this woman in her late thirties, hospitalized after a severe relapse of multiple sclerosis. The disease was progressing quickly, robbing her of mobility and independence. She had to give up her job, and her husband was struggling to balance work with caregiving. Her demeanor during the intake had been polite but distant, her eyes filled with exhaustion.

On impulse, I went back to check on her. Her room was quiet with the faint glow of city lights coming through the window. She was sitting up in bed, staring out, a sketchbook resting untouched beside her. I noticed her hands trembling slightly and thought of the control she must have lost.

"Do you mind if I sit for a bit?" I asked softly, and she nodded. Gesturing to the sketchbook, I said, "I see you draw. Do you still get a chance to?"

She shook her head. "My hands … they don't really listen to me anymore." Her voice was low, but I could hear the pain beneath her words.

I resisted the urge to offer empty comfort and instead reflected her feelings back. "It sounds like drawing is a big part of who you are. Losing that must feel like losing a piece of yourself."

Her eyes welled up, and she looked at me for a long moment before whispering, "Yes. Exactly."

We sat in silence, and I could feel the tension in her shoulders ease just a bit. Before I left, I told her, "If you ever want to talk, I'm here."

Her small smile was filled with gratitude. "Thank you. I didn't realize how much I needed this."

That experience is another example that reflectively listening is a fundamental component of being more emotionally intelligent. Medicine trains us to treat symptoms and find solutions, but sometimes the best care we can offer is simply being present, acknowledging pain without rushing to fix it. Sometimes what a patient needs most is to be seen, heard, and understood. In those quiet moments, healing happens in ways that medicine alone can't provide.

Sometimes it is easy to become so focused on our own thoughts and agendas that we overlook the silent stories written on the faces of those around us. Sometimes we hear but don't listen. We fail to hear their spoken words as well as what their body language is screaming. A furrowed brow, a tight smile, or distant eyes can speak of stress, sadness, or disengagement, yet often we miss these cues while caught up in our own narratives. A conversation is more than an exchange of information; it's an interaction rich with emotional subtext. We might be speaking, convinced that we are effectively communicating, yet fail to notice the listener's glazed eyes or impatient gestures that signal we are not being heard.

The ability to connect with people hinges on being astute observers, not just of what is said but of how it is said and received. It involves listening with our eyes and hearts as well as our ears, cultivating an awareness that is beyond mere words. This mindfulness allows us to read the room, gauge the emotional temperature, and respond in ways that foster genuine understanding and empathy. By developing this sensitivity, we enhance our capacity for empathy and strengthen our relationships, creating an environment in which everyone feels seen, heard, and valued.

We all long for the human connection. We desire to be heard. We may be a species with big brains, but we all react first with our hearts. How often have you not been able to make any logical sense of something vital in your life—falling in love (whether with the "right" or the "wrong" person), falling out of love, losing someone, feeling stuck? But let's face it—expressing emotions can be hard. What should be a relatively straightforward conversation with a work colleague when you feel they have overstepped or taken credit for work you did—but those are emotions we lose sleep over, right?

We all long for the human connection. We desire to be heard. We may be a species with big brains, but we all react first with our hearts.

We have to become masters of our EQ if we are going to have healthy, productive, reciprocal connections, whether at work or in our personal lives. Let's break it down and highlight a few things we can all do to improve our EQ.

Self-Awareness

It all starts, like so many things, with our own self-awareness. First, we need to figure out who we are. What do we value? Do we tend to lean into certain kinds of people or particular kinds of thinking? What sets us off? We all have to learn our trigger points, those things that push our buttons and make us say things we later regret or that are open to misinterpretation.

And because we are all different personality types, some personalities just don't blend. We are naturally like oil and water. It's not purposeful. Okay, typically it's not, although we all know people who intentionally trick us into losing our self-control. Usually, it's not even conscious. But we have to *become* conscious of the personalities and habits that grate against our nerves so that we can step back, take a breath, and recognize that the person who so easily seems to create a reaction in us probably has a valid, even valuable idea or contribution.

When we're triggered, we become instinctual beings and react with the oldest parts of our brains. The amygdala reduces us to our animal selves; we become the proverbial deer caught in the headlights and *freeze*, we become the mama bear protecting her cubs and *fight*, or we become the bird startled by the predator and take *flight*. I call it thinking from the basement because the amygdala is located in the base of the brain.

The thing is, we have all the other parts of our brains too. We don't have to go to the basement. Self-awareness can lead to self-regulation. We just have to teach ourselves to be open to hearing it. We can train ourselves to step back from a situation, to withdraw from something that has triggered our emotions.

I tell people, "Hold on—I'm thinking from my basement. Give me a minute."

Maybe I need five seconds, maybe five minutes, or maybe I need to sleep on it.

If we are not self-aware, we can become guilty of unconscious bias—in either direction—and miss useful insights or harm what could be productive relationships. I'm not saying we have to make accommodations for every person or every action every time, but we have to know ourselves well enough to know our blind spots.

Decoding Human Nature

Just think about the power of a smile. Don't you know someone who can change the aura of a whole room or make someone feel like they've really been seen with a genuine moment of eye contact accompanied by a smile? People want to be seen and heard. We have to learn how to listen, really listen. To acknowledge that we are listening. It's not just about listening with our ears; we need to be keenly observant, read people's expressions and body language as well, see what makes them excited or what shuts them down. We can't really expand our own EQ if we aren't capable of reading other people's emotions. So we can't be distracted when working with others, and we can't let interference come between us.

I see connection failures between people all the time. The factors that contribute are equally present in most workplaces—insufficient time, too heavy a workload, technology that creates interference, complicated bureaucracy.

As a clinician and a teacher, I often observe the inability of some doctors to connect with patient emotions or acknowledge their vulnerabilities. Often, doctors and nurses spend the whole time typing on the computer during a patient encounter and hardly make eye contact.

The question might be "On a scale of one to ten, how is your back pain?"

And even if the response is "This is the most excruciating pain of my life," the doctor is too busy dutifully typing away without ever engaging with their patient or acknowledging their pain, even just by saying, "I know—this must hurt." There's no eye contact. No emphatic reply to their physical pain. No acknowledgment of the emotion that accompanies it. We at times forget we are not taking a poll, that we are here to heal not only with medications but with our words.

We have to break down those walls and connect with the person before us. Even if it is a simple thing, noticing something about their appearance, work they have done, a potential shared interest, anything that allows us to meet one another on a human level and then to gauge their state of being. And scan yourself while you're at it:

"Decoding" the Encounter

- Are their arms folded?
- Will they hold your gaze?
- Do they answer your questions in a meaningful way?
- Are you leaning toward the person?
- Have you removed objects that would keep you at a distance?
- Have you used the simple, sincere gestures of human connection like a platonic touch or handshake?
- Do you maintain eye contact as they speak?
- Are you monitoring the pitch of your tone (a monotonous tone can be divisive)? Just changing your pitch can be soothing. Only by reading others and yourself can you create a space where connection can happen.

Reading the Room

Learning to read people as individuals helps prepare us to learn to read people as a group. How many times have you drifted off during an endless PowerPoint presentation (DPP: death by PowerPoint) or cringed when a speaker clearly didn't know anything about the makeup of the audience before them? There are so many times I start a presentation and look around the room to see that nobody cares about that particular topic; they are eager to address their own agenda. That's where being nimble and able to pivot can save your day.

You can go from being superdud to superhero if you learn to pivot. Sometimes the material is golden and the audience really should have interest, but the approach just isn't working. Or maybe they just ate a big lunch and want a nap or some bit of juicy gossip has everyone distracted. Or maybe you've experienced a meeting or a presentation where people are on their phones or laptops. Kind of like the doctor-patient scenario; they might tell you they are multitasking, but that's bunk. They're not really paying attention.

Rather than interrupting the session and putting them into fight or flight by asking them, "Why are you on the phone?" turn to the person next to them or behind them who is paying attention and ask their opinion about your last point. And 100 percent of the time, the culprit will put the phone down.

Why they are disengaged matters only as much as your ability to recognize that is the case, shift direction, and find a new way to bring them into the present moment. In the case of my phone example, I've not only solved the immediate problem; I've done so in a way that doesn't cause embarrassment—I've practiced a bit of EQ. You can't do that without self-awareness or other awareness either. And by the way, I've certainly been guilty of not paying close enough attention in meetings. Learning is constant.

Reflective Listening

Reading someone is important to give them space so they feel they can communicate. But then you actually have to listen. Not like your kids when you call them to dinner. We have to train ourselves to listen with the whole of our being, the way we absorb music we love. Listening has to become hearing. It is so difficult—the hardest ambition of mine to achieve.

I regularly use an exercise with my audience during teaching sessions. It aims to get them to practice an intentional habit in order to improve reflective listening. I ask people to split into pairs, and then one person is directed to speak for ninety seconds. The person who is the listener is only allowed to either nod their head or offer simple encouragement to demonstrate that they are hearing, using terms like *okay* or *I see*.

Sounds simple, right? But listening without interruption for ninety seconds is actually a lot harder than you would guess. I often hear this comment: "I wanted to interrupt so badly." On the other hand, most of the speakers comment after the exercise that they felt heard and that the practice is almost cathartic.

Studies in my field reveal that on average, physicians interrupt patients after eighteen seconds.[20] Eighteen seconds—I mean, come on! You have to stay on a rodeo bull for eight seconds; we can't do better than eighteen seconds? Talk about impatience. Because what

---

20 I. Plug, S. van Dulmen, W. Stommel, T. C. Olde Hartman, and E. Das, "Physicians' and Patients' Interruptions in Clinical Practice: A Quantitative Analysis," *Annals of Family Medicine* 20, no. 5 (September–October 2022): 423-429.

are we thinking in those eighteen seconds? *Okay, I've got this. Boom. Diagnosed and moving on.*

Acknowledging Emotion

Sometimes, if we are to understand someone, we've got to ask them to open up. We may have to ask them how they feel. Maybe not in the heat of the moment. Maybe not in the ER when patients are lined up. Maybe not in the boardroom when a proposal has been shot down. But circle back. As part of understanding what has occurred, find out what the person was feeling.

Were they angry? Frustrated? Scared? Were you? You might have to ask questions to elicit a response. And how did we respond, or how are we responding now? With compassion? With anger? With a desire to understand what the primary driver is for the other person? Is it fear, is it personal, or is it maybe their desire to be right?

Our objective may be to make a rational decision or implement a logical solution, but if the process of doing so has stirred emotion as well, we need to acknowledge that that emotion exists, not so much as a desire to change course but to create connection so that people believe they have a role in charting that course. That they are more than automatons.

Critical Conversations

It is always a defining moment how we handle ourselves when emotions are high and we have opposing views. Do we become argumentative, or do we give each other some space mixed with grace? Do we make people feel safe when things are tough? As a doctor, I may not immediately have all the answers when I have a complicated patient and must manage their concerns and those of their family.

It's not always possible, but if I don't have the answers I need, I always acknowledge that, try to explain why, and lead them with facts and observations rather than conclusions and emotions. I assure them about the next steps. If one can bring safety into a discussion, then most of the time people are more open to suggestions and alternatives. As a businessperson, sometimes there is an equivalent, where either I need more information to make a decision, need to stew on my thoughts for a bit, or simply acknowledge that "I've heard you," even if I'm going another way. It's always about cementing a connection.

Perhaps it requires a heartfelt apology. Maybe it's recognizing that there is a disagreement and discussing how to avoid a repeat. Sometimes it's just the empathy of recognizing the situation. When I must tell a patient of a cancer diagnosis, I tell them that "I'm sorry you are going through this."

It is important that we express our empathy. Empathy, not sympathy. Empathy is "I can feel for you what you're going through." Sympathy is "Look at that homeless guy sitting in the freezing cold; I pity him."

It boils down to maintaining awareness and control when the stakes are high, emotions are intense, and opposing views collide. Critical conversations happen in these challenging moments, where the goal is not just to communicate but to bridge divides and reach mutual understanding. During these exchanges, the most important components are creating a sense of safety, practicing reflective listening, and grounding the discussion in facts. Providing safety allows each person to speak openly without fear of judgment, while reflective listening ensures that everyone feels heard and validated. By focusing on facts over assumptions, participants can navigate emotionally charged topics more constructively and work toward a resolution that respects everyone's perspective.

All these approaches to enhancing your EQ are learnable skills. It starts with the desire to learn them. I once had a colleague, one of the smartest people I know when it comes to facts and numbers but who has limited EQ. Without even realizing it, he often said things to people that embarrassed them or sometimes even removed their sense of identity. So as a gift, I gave him a book on EQ.

His response was "Why are you giving this to me?"

"That's exactly my point, dude," I replied.

EQ starts with an awareness that it matters. Then it takes practice. Lots of practice.

I would implore you to go and search for an online EQ test. One resource could be the Institute for Health and Human Potential (IHHP) EQ Test (search for "IHHP EQ Test"). Your results could be quite revealing.

By intentionally developing these aspects of emotional intelligence, I have become better equipped to understand and respond to the needs and emotions of those around me. This has not only improved my personal relationships but has also enriched my life with deeper connections and greater mutual respect and understanding.

Growing your EQ in the ways I have outlined is like a brainteaser for your emotions. It will help your relationships with your colleagues, your friends, and your family members. Remember, people across wide swaths of Asia trained elephants to be like modern-day bulldozers and semitrucks and logging cranes. Their riders learned how to appeal to them in ways that put them to work; they figured out how to communicate with them. Sure, there will be times our "elephant" will go on a rampage, but we have big brains that we can train to open our hearts.

WEIGHT OF SUCCESS

This black-and-white photograph captures a vintage apothecary or spice shop in Sarasota, Florida, its shelves lined with jars and containers filled with herbs, spices, and mysterious ingredients. The image suggests that success is not simply found or given; it is earned through a careful balance of inputs, decisions, and dedication, just as the shop owner might measure each herb with intention and precision.

The serene, almost meditative atmosphere of the shop serves as a reminder that achieving balance is key. Ultimately, we pause a bit to consider what we're willing to invest—and what we may need to give up—to tip the scales in our favor.

CHAPTER 10
Success: Check the Price Tag

Success is the progressive realization of a worthy goal or ideal. But remember, you have to pay the price in advance and in full.
—EARL NIGHTINGALE

Life teaches us perspective in a staggering way. Only with time are we allowed to self-reflect and gather some wisdom. When it comes to how we measure success, we certainly need perspective, for quite often the price affiliated with arriving at success gets overshadowed. Achieving success isn't a stroll in the park. Success can be a demanding deity, asking for sacrifices along the way.

While I, like you, set high expectations for myself in many of the conventional ways of defining success, I've learned the hard way that it is crucial not to let the pursuit of success overshadow everything else in life. While aiming for your goals, be mindful not to lose sight of the things that bring joy and fulfillment. Those will keep you grounded and provide the foundation required for trying to reach goals and dreams. Do the work you value with passion and commitment, but don't sacrifice everything on the altar of success.

There are plenty of historical examples of people we view as pillars of success that should give us pause. We often hold such people up as models, but have we looked behind the curtain?

Abraham Lincoln is revered as one of the greatest US presidents, leading the nation through the fracture of the American Civil War and issuing the Emancipation Proclamation to free slaves. But after his son Willie died, he suffered strained family relationships and fell into bouts of melancholy, leading him in his own time to be known as "the man of sorrows."[21]

His marriage to Mary Todd Lincoln was marked by challenges, for she struggled with mental health issues all her life. Even on the political front, his stances were nuanced, for while he ultimately issued a proclamation to free slaves and found slavery morally reprehensible, his primary goal in fighting the Civil War was to preserve the Union, not to end slavery. He avoided public comments that connected the war to the rights of slaves.

Winston Churchill played a pivotal role in leading the United Kingdom during World War II, earning him historical acclaim as a great wartime leader such that in 2002 he beat out figures like Shakespeare and Darwin as the "greatest Briton" in public polls.[22] Yet he was labeled as an irreconcilable imperialist in his views toward India and his inflammatory attacks on Ghandi. Like Lincoln, Churchill struggled with personal issues. He faced financial difficulties, suffered numerous health problems, coped with bouts of depression (which he famously

---

21 H. I. Smith, "Abraham Lincoln: A Man of Sorrows and Acquainted with Grief," *Illness, Crisis & Loss* 32, no. 2 (2024): 329–355, https://doi.org/10.1177/10541373221143686.

22 "Winston Churchill—The Greatest Briton," Parliament UK, March 2014, https://www.parliament.uk/globalassets/documents/parliamentary-archives/Churchill-for-web-Mar-2014.pdf.

referred to as the "black dog"), and experienced political setbacks tied to his treatment of striking union workers, Jews, and Muslims.[23]

Pablo Picasso revolutionized the art world with his innovative and influential contributions to modern art, cofounding the cubist movement, while his personal life was marked by tumultuous relationships. He had multiple marriages and often faced criticism for his treatment of women, including his muses. His intense focus on his art sometimes strained his connections with those close to him.

Similarly, Frida Kahlo is celebrated for her unique and iconic art, exploring themes of identity, pain, and Mexican culture, yet she endured a tumultuous marriage to fellow artist Diego Rivera. Both Kahlo and Rivera had extramarital affairs, contributing to the complexities of their relationship. Additionally, Kahlo's health struggles and physical pain were constant companions throughout her life.

We could go on and on citing many more examples of "successful" people who are household names. Success does not automatically mean happiness. Successful people often experience failures in various aspects of their lives, demonstrating that achievement in one area doesn't shield them from setbacks in another. A few common themes can be seen—strained relationships and poor health and well-being (mental health is a big one).

Not only have many "successful" people struggled with other aspects of their lives, many were considered failures for long periods before realizing success. History is replete with stories of individuals who were initially considered failures but were later recognized as tremendously successful, their legacies enduring and inspiring. If we look back in the history of some of the most renowned people and

---

23 W. Dockter and A. Packwood, *Churchill's Contested History*, in *The Cambridge Companion to Winston Churchill*, ed. A. Packwood, Cambridge Companions to History (series) (Cambridge University Press, 2023), 11–27.

study only a portion of their lives, our conclusion would not be that these are successful people. Far from it.

Walt Disney was fired from a newspaper for "a lack of imagination" and "having no good ideas."[24],[25] Had we stopped there, there would be no Disney, a pioneer in American animation and the founder of a global entertainment empire. J. K. Rowling initially lived on welfare, and she was rejected by twelve publishers before finding a home for her work; she later became one of the most successful and beloved authors in the world. My personal favorite "failure" is Van Gogh, who suffered from mental illness to the extent that he famously mutilated his own ear. Today he would probably be homeless and on drugs, yet because of the art he produced, he is now considered one of the greatest painters of all time, and his works command millions of dollars at auctions.

These individuals exemplify that failure is often a stepping stone to success. Their stories highlight resilience, perseverance, and the unyielding pursuit of passion, reminding us that success is not defined by how many times you fall but by how many times you get back up.

What Is Success?

So what does it mean to succeed? Real success is found in shared victories, while selfish success is little more than an empty triumph. Otherwise, there will be some causalities, either poor health, strained

---

24 "Walt Disney: Fired from His Job at a Newspaper Because He Was "Not Creative," Business | ArcaMax Publishing, October 25, 2024, https://www.arcamax.com/business/workplace101/s-2848028; "The Story of a Man Who Was Fired for a Lack of Creativity but Went On to Build His Own Empire," Bright Side, https://brightside.me/articles/the-story-of-a-man-who-was-fired-for-a-lack-of-creativity-but-went-on-to-build-his-own-empire-798520/?utm_source=chatgpt.com.

25

relationships, or compromised well-being. Success is a multifaceted concept that varies widely in definition depending on personal values, cultural influences, and individual goals.

The meaning of success can range from financial achievements and professional accolades to personal fulfillment and positive impact on society. As we strive for success, it is beneficial to remember that enriching one dimension of our lives should not come at the expense of others. Balancing these aspects is not only achievable but necessary for true holistic success, providing a more satisfying and sustainable path to personal fulfillment.

Success is a high-stakes game, where the roll of the dice could bring triumph or tribulation.

Success is often achieved by the sweat, tears, and sacrifices of those who dare to aspire to difficult goals. The characters in this narrative stand in the spotlight, their faces etched with the lines of resilience and determination. What we don't see in the dark recesses of the stage are the moments of missed family and friends, the late nights, the myriad disappointments, and the weight of responsibilities carried. The audience applause may be thunderous, but the actor in the spotlight wears scars of sacrifice underneath their makeup. Success is a high-stakes game, where the roll of the dice could bring triumph or tribulation. The factors at play are diverse—hard work, resilience, sacrifice, and a dash of luck—all dancing in unpredictable harmony.

Pain or sacrifice may not accompany every accomplishment, but relentless hard work and commitment most certainly will. We may not all face clear offsets for our success the way these historical examples have, but it is still useful to think of success for most of us as compartmentalized. When I look at myself, I've been successful in some ways, but I've failed miserably in a lot of other things.

In some of the periods when I labored through the most hours of "furthering my career," I lost connection with the people I love most, and I most certainly was not happy. I have shared my trying times in finding a job and finally when I first arrived in Tampa. I was fueled by eagerness, ambition, and a thirst for knowledge. I was on a mission to work the hardest, learn the most, and create something different. Days and nights blurred. It was easy to dismiss it all as being the normal part of a doctor's life. I was fixated on what I thought I wanted to "accomplish."

When we think about success, we tend to think about the destination when it's all about the journey. In fact, the destination rarely stays the same. The goalposts for how we measure our own success are always moving. What was once a paramount goal may transform with time.

Think about it. How often have you fought and fought to achieve something, and the moment you accomplish that something, you want something more? Think about a very simple example: when you've been desperately looking forward to a vacation you've been planning for a long time, you start to miss home the moment you leave. Wanting more—that's part of the price tag of being successful.

Sometimes, our drive to succeed stems from the wrong motivations. It could be due to our insecurities, a feeling of not being enough, or an emptiness we're desperate to fill. Perhaps we're trying to prove to others that we've made it, but in doing so, we risk losing ourselves. In our quest for acceptance, we might forget what truly brings us joy and what makes us who we are.

The other reality about success is that it is always subjective. What you deem success to be and what I believe it to be probably aren't the same. As we try to navigate our success journey, we draw an intricate map filled with individual values and evolving aspirations.

Societal or cultural perspectives and expectations also play vital roles in defining success. In some cultures, the conventional measure of success is monetary. In others, success can be viewed as having influence. Just as we might all define success differently, we probably disagree on what makes us happy.

Maybe the pursuit of happiness is a noble way to look at success. In my native Pakistan, while I came from the big city of Karachi, like a lot of places much of the country is made up of small villages where people are simple sustenance farmers. Often in such villages, you can encounter elders who are extremely respected, and their lives tend to be focused on family, community, and very simple pleasures. They laugh a lot. They spend a lot of time with friends while sipping chai.

They have very few material possessions, but they are happy. They may have never left their hometown. They didn't invent Tesla. They don't post photos of meals on social media. They don't have gender-reveal parties, nor do they carry Gucci bags. They simply apply a different measure of success—the happiness they experience. They live by different cultural values. Are they right and we're wrong? Are we right and they're wrong? We just have different expectations, and some of us are winning in life.

Finding Balance

Both societal and personal expectations can leave us struggling to find a balance in our lives. I've frequently found myself caught between competing expectations. Balance doesn't just happen. We have to become intentional about establishing balance. Intentional as opposed to having good intentions. All my life I had good intentions. It didn't always work out. But when I act with intentionality, I can make change happen.

For example, I don't get to see patients with the frequency I used to, although it remains one of the most satisfying parts of my professional life when I do. My time in hospital rooms attending to patients is limited because I now have several other corporate responsibilities and manage hundreds of people. So my time management issues haven't gone away. If anything, I have far more responsibilities, including those to all the people who work with me.

But in the process of becoming a "boss" (I hate that *B* word), I've matured in certain parts of my life. That includes being intentional in how I achieve balance. I've taken measures to leave work behind when I am home and be fully present—both physically and, more significantly, mentally. I've chosen, after hard lessons, to place my family first. I've also found the personal "therapies" that keep me whole, creative, and happy. Those include art and the yearly skills exploration I've spoken of already.

Throughout my life, I've always had a deep love for both medicine and the arts. Cultivation of both has always resonated within me. When facing even the most critical patients, I approached the challenge akin to a painter before a canvas, with a tuned heart, slowed time, focused eyes, and an imaginative mind. When I interact with patients, I aim to make them feel safe, seen, and heard. Through meticulous observation and examination, I leverage my medical knowledge to chart the best course for them. I truly try to make medicine an art, and at times art is my medicine. Find yours—it's the best therapy.

And I use my time—time that is as precious to me as any other—creating art, whether that is painting, drawing, sculpting, or building furniture, as a means to de-stress from work. Mostly, practicing art is just something that suits me, as natural to me as breathing, but when you pass your workdays in the presence of disease and death and difficult problems (and health and life and solutions to be sure), I have found the act of creation to be a powerful self-healing tool.

Medicine is an art. The interrelationship between art and medicine is a fascinating study of how two seemingly distinct disciplines influence and enrich each other. At its core, medicine involves the science of healing, but it is also an art that requires practitioners to engage empathetically and creatively with their patients. Similarly, art not only seeks to provoke and inspire but also to heal and provide solace, often playing a therapeutic role in medical settings. Conversely, the precision and empirical rigor of medicine influence artistic expression by providing insights into the human condition, anatomy, and the physiological processes of life and death.

When you connect these dots, you get an astute clinician. I have met some really skilled surgeons; their work is like that of a master artist, coiling those secretly hidden brain aneurysms or literally separating the heart from the body to replace it with artificial heart devices, but some of them look so unhappy. They are successful at what they do, and on the contrary, some of them are just sad people.

In this dance between personal aspirations and societal expectations, the key may lie in aligning one's definition of success with intrinsic values. Success is more than mere material wealth; it encompasses a holistic sense of accomplishment and contentment. Practicing creativity, whether in the production of art or the application of a new process in a hospital system, is one of my values. Yours are different.

In this dance between personal aspirations and societal expectations, the key may lie in aligning one's definition of success with intrinsic values.

Aligning a personal definition of success with one's own intrinsic values involves embracing the evolving nature of goals, understanding the trade-offs, and cultivating a sense of fulfillment in the present rather than postponing happiness to a distant future. As is common in Eastern belief systems and increasingly true in Western ones, many have come to see that our only control lies in the present; the past is beyond our influence, and we can shape our future by our actions in the present. Success isn't a dash to the finish; it's a marathon, measured in miles and moments. Each step is a small victory, each mile a chapter, unfolding slowly as you go.

Success is a symphony of choices, risks, and sacrifices. I am not at all dissuading anyone from striving for success. I love ambitious people. I am one. We just need to alter our perception of success to avoid some of the pitfalls along the way. Success comes at a price, and the journey demands a thoughtful consideration of the sacrifices involved. That means contemplating the shadows and highlights of the journey—a poignant tableau of the price paid for a seat in the hall of success.

In the end, ask yourself this: "How do I define success?" To me, the truest form of success is mutual success, while the worst kind is selfish success. Shared success creates lasting value and has a much longer shelf life. But beyond that, how does success make you feel? Does it bring you happiness, a sense of accomplishment, and pride in your achievements? Or does it leave behind a trail of casualties, where the cost of your success feels more like bloodshed? In the end, take a moment to pause and think about what success means to you and what its price is—it may give you deeper insight into the kind of success you're really striving for.

FURIA EN LOS CENOTE

I captured this image as I was walking toward a cenote in Belize. It perfectly captures the spider monkey's raw expression of frustration as the monkey lets out a scream, bound by a rope around its neck. The rope represents the emotional state–restricted by its circumstances, obligations, or expectations. The intense anger, helplessness, and frustration on its face are emotions often felt by leaders who, despite their roles, feel constrained and powerless, caught in a cycle of responsibilities that no longer align with their purpose or well-being.

Just as the monkey is visibly caught between fury and a desire for freedom, leaders must confront their own traps, recognizing when they're bound by self-imposed constraints or toxic expectations. Only by acknowledging these restraints can they regain control, reconnect with their purpose, and find their way back to the peaceful, restorative waters of their own cenotes.

CHAPTER 11

Leadership Traps: Avoiding Self-inflicted Failure

The greatest trap for a leader is believing that the same qualities that elevated them cannot also destroy them.
—LIVIA MORRELL, THE PARADOX OF POWER

Let me tell you about someone I'll call "Dr. Smith," the big shot in one of our hospitals a few years back. This guy was like a storm rolling through the healthcare corridors. He wasn't a leader—he was a tyrant, a bully disguised in a white coat ruling through intimidation rather than inspiration. He had a knack for ruffling feathers and making enemies faster than you could say "stethoscope." Even the way he looked at you made you shrink inside, as if his cold, piercing gaze could strip away your confidence and reduce you to nothing.

Now, don't get me wrong. Dr. Smith was brilliant, no doubt about that. But his people skills? Bedside manner? Let's just say they were on life support. Patient care? It was all about the numbers and statistics for him. The guy was more interested in filling hospital beds than connecting with patients.

He had a habit of bulldozing over everyone—nurses, fellow doctors, even the custodial staff. Nobody was safe from his tempestuous reign. He had an uncanny ability to turn even the simplest meetings into battlefields. You'd think twice before suggesting anything, because chances were you'd end up on the receiving end of his infamous scowl.

But what made him totally unbearable was his tendency to take all the credit. You'd bust your butt on a project, and when it came time for recognition, he'd swoop in like a healthcare superhero claiming he'd single-handedly saved the day. As you can imagine, the staff turnover rate skyrocketed under his watch. Nurses were polishing their résumés, doctors were sending out feelers to other hospitals, and even the cafeteria staff were contemplating early retirement.

In the end, Dr. Smith's leadership style caught up with him. The hospital board had had enough of the internal wars and the plummeting morale. They showed him the door faster than you could say "malpractice." So, there you have it: Dr. Smith, the healthcare leader who could diagnose diseases but had no cure for his own toxic leadership. Sometimes brilliance in one area doesn't excuse a lack of compassion in another.

The day he was leaving, he said to another colleague, "I don't understand why I am being fired." I remember reflecting that it's all right to admit what you don't know—awareness is the first step to growth. But it's dangerous to be blind to your own ignorance, for that is where true mistakes are born. Those are the kinds of self-imposed failures from which you can't recover.

The Pitfalls of Leadership

Leadership is a double-edged sword. It demands self-sacrifice, but the rewards can be fulfilling. It comes with its pitfalls of sleepless nights, overwork, and extreme responsibility. The buck really does stop here, sometimes with a jarring screech and leaving behind only a pounding migraine. Leadership is not something to be taken lightly or entered into for reasons of self-aggrandizement.

The pitfalls of leaders who merely pursue leadership titles for the sake of vanity are deep and muddy. There exists a profound distinction between those who lead because it is required to uplift others or better the larger organization versus those who merely seek the title as a crown for their ego. First, true leaders build their foundation with hard work and selfless dedication; they are driven to grow and improve themselves. Second, they are motivated to create something meaningful that enhances the lives of others. They demonstrate selfless dedication.

For leaders like Dr. Smith, leadership is merely a hollow title worn as an accessory to their professional image. These leaders, driven by a desire for status rather than substance, often lack the essential qualities that define true leadership. These sorts of leaders eventually find themselves isolated and trapped.

A title earned without dedication and authentic purpose is like a castle built on shifting sands, vulnerable to the winds of change and the erosion of trust; a good leader must not only recognize the tools at their disposal but also understand what they still need to acquire, including emotional intel-

A title earned without dedication and authentic purpose is like a castle built on shifting sands, vulnerable to the winds of change and the erosion of trust.

ligence, clear communication, strategic vision, authenticity, adaptability, and the ability to build connections.

The dark hours unveil the fragility of leadership that lacks a solid footing in merit and dedication. In contrast, authentic leaders who have earned their titles through diligent effort and the creation of value remain resilient even in the darkest times, regardless of the ground they stand on. Whether in moments of stability or crisis, their authenticity inspires trust, and people continue to rely on them. Their leadership is not a facade but a beacon that illuminates the path for others. They shoulder responsibility, make meaningful contributions, and lead selflessly in times of need. Leadership, like respect, must be earned.

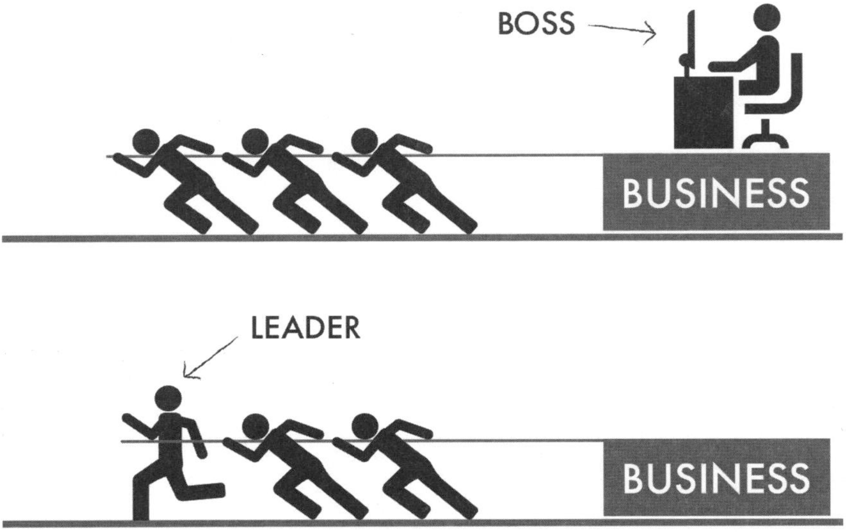

At Pioneer, I don't have a private office; I sit in a cubicle among colleagues. Some assume I do this to keep an eye on things, but the truth is quite the opposite. I choose to sit there because I believe it fosters a better connection with the people around me. The same principle guided me when I worked in healthcare—I never liked to eat in the physician lounges. Instead, I preferred to have my meals in the cafeteria, and I did my notes at the nursing station rather than tucked away in a dictation room. Authentic, genuine relationships can only be built when you're present with others, not set apart on a pedestal. For me, leadership is about creating those real connections—it's about being accessible, relatable, and human.

As I write these words, I'm reminded of a conversation with a doctor years ago. On his first day of work, with a sense of entitlement, he boldly stated, "I demand the same respect from the staff as they show you."

A pregnant pause filled the room before I calmly responded, "There are two ways to get that. I could send a memo to the staff, or ... you could try to earn it."

Leadership is not a royal decree; it is a calling. Many remarkable leaders didn't assert their leadership; they embraced it when the calling arose. Their ascent was marked by the acknowledgment that roles hold more significance than titles. Occasionally, we become entangled in our titles, losing sight of the essence of our roles. However, the truths about leadership are things I did not always know—they were hard-earned lessons I had to learn over time.

In fact, there was a period when I might not have sounded so different from the doctor I hired, carrying similar expectations. There were times in my career when I believed that holding a prestigious title would automatically bring both professional success and personal fulfillment. I thought a lofty designation like "chief of something" would secure my rise to more prominent positions and earn me respect simply because of the role I held.

All it does is pull you away—like a ship drifting from the harbor, like a bird straying too far from the flock, or like a leaf drifting from its tree—severed from the wholeness that gives life meaning. No matter how skilled you are at navigating the rat race, at the end of the day, even if you win, you're still a rat. Real leadership is about authenticity, humility, and building meaningful connections. It's about earning respect through actions, not demanding it because of rank.

Leadership, at its core, is a journey fraught with traps that can entangle you. Each leader, like a ship's captain staring into the horizon, must learn to navigate through a myriad of traps that threaten to destabilize their course. These traps—subtle, yet powerful—can ensnare even the most seasoned leaders, pulling them into the mire of ineffective leadership. Here are some of the leadership traps I have observed too many times:

Leadership Traps

- **Self-Awareness Fog:** A lack of self-awareness disconnects leaders from their impact on others; leaders become blind to their strengths and unwilling to face their limitations.
- **Sirens of Perfection and Impulsivity:** Two opposing forces—a mythical quest for perfection that creates analysis paralysis and reactive thinking for immediate response.
- **The Chameleon's Mask:** Imposter syndrome is the belief that you don't belong in a leadership position, trapped by doubt and hiding behind facades that erode genuine confidence.
- **Quicksand of Ego and Illusion of Control**: What happens when unchecked confidence morphs into ego; the more you seek control, the more you sink into self-deception.
- **Abyss of Black-and-White Thinking**: The inability to manage nuance and complexity; rigid extremes blind you to the vibrant spectrum of possibilities.
- **Flow Like Water**: Embrace change; strength comes from flexibility—learn to flow, not resist.
- **The Bridge of Clarity**: Leadership communication—leadership is built on clear, authentic words that inspire and connect.
- **Mastering the Basement**: The power of self-control—true leadership shines in restraint, choosing actions over impulsive reactions.

Self-Awareness Fog

The first and perhaps most treacherous trap a leader can fall into is lack of self-awareness. Like walking through a thick mist, a leader who lacks self-awareness is disconnected from their own motivations, behaviors, and the impact they have on others. This blindness often leads to misjudgments and can alienate a leader from their team. In such a fog, decisions are made based on misconceptions, assumptions, or personal biases, which only further clouds the path forward.

Self-awareness is not only about understanding one's strengths but also about acknowledging one's limitations. A lack of this awareness can turn a once-promising leader into someone out of touch with their followers. To escape this fog, leaders must cultivate honest self-reflection, seek feedback, and maintain a willingness to grow from their mistakes. Only then can they regain clarity. This leads to the concept of "pluses equal to minuses."

This concept represents a continuous journey of self-improvement: recognizing your strengths and enhancing them plus acknowledging your weaknesses and working to reduce them. The end result is balance—still equal, but in a stronger, better version of yourself.

This is a powerful tool for self-improvement and self-awareness by helping you embrace balance, understand trade-offs, and cultivate a realistic view of yourself and the world. Here's how you can apply it.

First, acknowledge your strengths and weaknesses. Every strength has a corresponding challenge or potential downside. Being detail oriented (a plus) might make you prone to overthinking (a minus). Similarly, being spontaneous (a plus) could lead to impulsivity (a minus). For example, if you're highly analytical but slow to act, you can practice setting deadlines to balance thought and action.

Understanding trade-offs can help you make intentional choices that align with your values and goals rather than feeling overwhelmed or regretful later. Question yourself: *What part of myself am I avoiding?* For example, if you're overly accommodating, explore where you might be suppressing assertiveness. By integrating both sides, you can live more authentically. Another example would be if you're overly focused on success, ask yourself if you're neglecting rest or relationships. Strive for harmony.

By applying the concept of "pluses equal to minuses," you can shift your perspective from striving for an impossible ideal to embracing balance and wholeness. This approach fosters self-acceptance, intentionality, and resilience, helping you grow into a more grounded and authentic version of yourself.

As you reflect on these concepts, you need to reflect on what type of a leader you want to be. Are you going to be a servant leader, a transactional leader only focused on rewards and punishment, an autocratic leader, or a delegate leader? I want you to pause, which is always the first step toward self-realization. It is important to figure this out.

This reminds me of a story from a dozen years ago. We were hosting a celebration—a welcome dinner for the new doctors joining our group, a chance for them to meet the leadership team, and for us to make a strong first impression. The restaurant, however, was far from impressive. It was small, dingy, and far too hot for comfort. The narrow conference room where we were gathered felt cramped, its dim lighting and outdated decor doing little to make up for the stuffy air. Even the ceiling fans, spinning lazily above us, couldn't keep the heat from settling into the room.

Still, we made the best of it. The CEO and chief medical officer of the hospital were seated at the head of the long, scratched wooden table, trying their best to maintain the upbeat tone of the evening. Around them were various department heads and senior physicians, me included. At the far end of the table sat the new doctors—some fresh from their residencies, brimming with ambition—some looking eager, others appearing slightly uneasy, and some seeming angry in the uncomfortable setting.

The conversation flowed in the usual manner, the kind of small talk typical of events like these. Introductions were made, stories of hospital life were shared, and expectations for the coming months were discussed. Then, all of a sudden it dawned on me that this group was not aware of what I was going to be discussing. Our understanding was that the group already knew that their employment would be changed from their current company to ours. What we didn't know was that that discussion had never happened with this group prior to our arrival.

I could sense a subtle tension in the room. Initially I thought maybe it was the oppressive heat or the fact that no one had quite anticipated how out of place we'd feel in this less-than-ideal restaurant. The tension reached a breaking point with the revelation that the hospital had recently entered into a contract with our company, and much to our surprise, one of the administrators made this announcement in front of us: "This group has the option to join our group or look for other options."

I was caught by surprise. This awkward disclosure amplified the uneasiness present in the room.

Among the new doctors, one stood out. He was tall, sharp looking, and had the kind of presence that suggested he was determined to prove himself. He'd been quiet most of the evening, but I could see the wheels turning in his mind. Although I could relate to his anger, I sensed this might not end well. That day was his first on the job after completing his residency. If I recall correctly, he hadn't even finished his first set of progress notes yet. When he heard the announcement, his brow furrowed and a flicker of surprise crossed his face.

As the conversation shifted to the realities of working with our group—new contracts, policies, procedures, and the subtle nuances that make every group unique—he stood up and rightfully said, "No one told me that I would be changing jobs."

I was already sweating with the revelation that this group had no idea until we showed up that they would be asked to work for us.

This new doctor, standing tall, looked directly at me from across the table and said, in a voice just loud enough for everyone to hear, "Well, I know what I bring to the table. What do you bring to the table? I trusted the executive who hired me. I don't know you at all." Despite the sharpness of his tone, I believed it was a fair statement.

The room fell silent. Even the soft hum of conversation from the main dining area outside seemed to fade. His words hung in the warm, stagnant air, and I could feel every eye in the room shift toward me. The CEO and CMO exchanged quick, unreadable glances. It was one of those moments—one where a single misstep could either escalate tension or open a path to understanding.

I could have responded in any number of ways. A part of me bristled at his confidence, or perhaps it was defensiveness rising within me. A dozen responses raced through my mind. I could have reminded him that confidence didn't trump experience or that adaptability was more important than certainty in a hospital setting. I could have used this as an opportunity to assert my authority in front of everyone and put him in his place.

But I was aware that I was losing my patience, and my self-awareness stopped me. I knew better than to react emotionally. This wasn't about a power struggle or about putting this person in his place. His words weren't an attack; they were more of a defense mechanism, a shield to mask the insecurity he truly felt in such an unfamiliar environment. He wanted to be seen as valuable, as someone worth investing in.

His confidence, while somewhat misplaced in the moment, came from a desire to prove himself, not to challenge me directly.

So, I took a deep breath, leaned back slightly in my chair, and gave him a calm, measured look. The room waited in that thick silence, the oppressive heat making every second feel longer.

"You're right," I said, my tone even, without a hint of aggression. "I need to prove what I can do for you."

The simplicity of my response took him by surprise. For a moment, his posture softened, the defensiveness in his expression easing. The tension in the room began to dissipate, the unease that had hung over the table like the restaurant's stuffy air starting to lift. My reply wasn't defensive or condescending; it was open, inviting collaboration instead of competition. It gave him the space to feel acknowledged without feeling diminished. Gradually, the conversation resumed. I'd diffused the situation without making it confrontational.

As the dinner concluded, I reflected on the exchange. It had been a test—one that many leaders face but not all pass. It would have been easy to react from a place of ego, to meet his confidence with my own, but self-control and self-awareness had shown me the bigger picture. Leadership isn't about proving who's in charge; it's about guiding others to reach their full potential. In that brief moment, I chose to create space for him to grow rather than shut him down. The ability to pause, reflect, and choose the response that will lead to growth rather than conflict is perhaps one of the most valuable skills a leader can possess.

And as we all stood to leave, brushing off the evening's discomfort and heat, I knew that this doctor had learned something too. Leadership isn't about what you bring to the table in terms of knowledge or skills alone—it's also about how you listen, how you respond, and how you navigate the unspoken dynamics in the room.

In time, this doctor grew into an exceptional leader, a wonderful entrepreneur—compassionate, organized, and ultimately guiding the team like a true champion. His bravado at the dinner where I first met him was tempered by the realization that he had entered a team, not a battlefield.

Over time I have developed tools that aid in solidifying self-awareness. I've always had a habit of using pen and paper to capture my ideas, strategies, and plans. For me, if it's not on paper, it doesn't exist. Writing things down solidifies them. Even in my conference room, I have glass walls, and I am constantly writing ideas on them. Doing so turns abstract thoughts into tangible action items, giving them life. There's something powerful about seeing ideas laid out in front of you, whether it's a complex strategy or a simple thought that needs refinement. The act of writing creates clarity and accountability, both for myself and for those I work with.

Along these same lines, I sometimes practice a plus-or-minus exercise that I encourage others to do as well. I create two columns on a sheet of paper. On one side, I write down my strengths, and on the other, my weaknesses. This simple exercise, done with pen in hand, offers deep insight into where we stand as leaders. It's not enough to simply know both; we must consciously work on both. Your strengths can become stronger, and your weaknesses can improve if you are aware of them and put in the effort to address them.

By visually laying out these aspects, I find it easier to see where my focus needs to be. It's not just a matter of enhancing your strengths or improving your weaknesses—both are equally important to develop if you want to achieve true growth. This awareness is a

> Leadership is also about how you listen, how you respond, and how you navigate the unspoken dynamics in the room.

key point I observe in myself and in others. When people have their strengths and weaknesses clearly written in front of them, it forces an honest self-assessment, one that often leads to actionable steps toward self-improvement.

By addressing your weaknesses, you can start identifying areas of struggle without judgment. Understand the root cause, set specific goals, and seek resources or feedback to guide your growth. Consistent practice and small, intentional steps turn weaknesses into strengths over time. Celebrate progress, reflect often, and view self-improvement as a lifelong journey.

Jotting down my thoughts with a pen and paper serves as a catalyst for accountability, reflection, and growth. This helps me turn thoughts into reality.

Sirens of Perfection and Impulsivity

PERFECTION

Much like the mythological sirens who lured sailors to their doom, perfectionism can draw leaders into an obsessive quest for flawlessness. This obsession not only paralyzes progress but also creates a culture of fear and anxiety within teams. The constant striving for an impossible ideal can stifle creativity and innovation, as both require room for trial, error, and learning. Perfectionism seduces with the promise of excellence but delivers frustration and burnout. Leaders who fall prey to this trap must learn that perfection is a moving target. Instead of seeking the impossible, they should strive for progress and foster an environment where mistakes are seen as learning opportunities rather than failures.

My mother loves telling this story about a conversation she had with a friend years ago. It always makes me smile because, like most things she says, it's simple but packs a punch. One day, this friend was going on about how she was *always* striving for perfection—how everything had to be just *so*, from her work projects down to the way her kitchen drawers were organized. She was practically chasing perfection like it was the last bus of the day.

My mom, with her usual calm, paused, thought for a moment, and then said something so classic that it has stuck with me ever since. She said, "I try to do the best I can, but I can't be perfect. Only God is perfect, and we are not."

Boom! It was one of those moments that felt like someone dropped the mic at a family dinner. And she wasn't wrong.

This, my friends, is one of the most important lessons in leadership—or in life, really. Sometimes we get so tangled up in the quest for a perfect solution, a perfect plan, and a perfect execution that we end up chasing our tails. We drown in months of meetings, endlessly debating every last detail. People get lost. It's like a ship sailing in circles because no one can decide on the *perfect* course to take. The result? Blind pursuit of perfection that leads to paralysis by analysis.

THE QUAGMIRE OF PARALYSIS BY ANALYSIS

Let's talk about that fun little place I like to call the quagmire of paralysis by analysis. You know the spot—it's that mental swamp where decisions go to die because you're so deep in overthinking that you can't see a way out. In stark contrast to those leaders who rush headlong into impulsive decisions, some leaders find themselves endlessly spinning their wheels, trying to make everything just right before taking a single step forward.

This is what happens when leaders get stuck in the pursuit of perfect information. They overanalyze every possible outcome, anticipate every possible risk, and nitpick every detail to death. And while they're waiting for 100 percent certainty (spoiler: it's never going to come), decisions are endlessly delayed. The result? Nothing happens.

It's a classic trap. You're afraid to make the wrong choice, so you make no choice at all—which, ironically, is a choice. It's the decision to do *nothing*. And in leadership, doing nothing can sometimes be worse than making the wrong call. At least with action, you learn something. But with inaction, you're just stuck in limbo, and your team is stuck right there with you, scratching their heads, wondering why no progress is being made.

Picture this. You're in a meeting. It's the third one this week on the same topic, and you're all discussing how to improve patient satisfaction. Many healthcare systems rely on surveys like HCAHPS (Hospital Consumer Assessment of Healthcare Providers and Systems) to measure patient satisfaction. While these metrics are useful, leaders can become too focused on boosting scores rather than addressing the underlying issues that truly matter to patients. This can lead to superficial changes, like making sure staff use "scripted phrases" or ensuring that patients are asked certain questions just to check a box, rather than focusing on the real patient experience.

For example, hospitals might invest in things like new pillows, improved waiting room aesthetics, or fancy new digital feedback systems. While these things can help, they don't always get to the root of what improves patient satisfaction—like effective communication, compassionate care, and efficient processes. It's easy to spend time and money on quick fixes or "nice-to-haves" while neglecting the more difficult systemic changes that patients notice most.

People often say, "The devil is in the details," suggesting that while something may seem simple on the surface, the complexity and potential problems often lie hidden in the finer points. This is especially true in leadership, project management, or any complex task. It's true that paying attention to the details is often what separates success from failure.

Imagine planning a major hospital expansion. The big picture seems clear: more rooms, more staff, better patient care. But if you overlook small details—like licensing requirements, safety regulations, or even proper staff scheduling—the entire project can falter. Details are where mistakes hide, and failure to spot them can lead to costly errors. In many cases, success hinges on thoroughness, precision, and the ability to foresee potential problems in those tiny details.

On the other hand, it's also true that we can overemphasize details at the expense of the big picture. While details are important, obsessing over them can result in paralysis by analysis—where decision-making is delayed because people get bogged down in minor issues. Focusing too much on perfection in every detail can prevent progress, stifle innovation, and delay necessary action. In leadership, it's often more valuable to make timely decisions and adapt along the way than to lose momentum trying to perfect every small aspect of a project.

While details are critical, it's equally important not to let them paralyze progress or overshadow the broader vision. Balance is key. Don't become the devil in the details rather than the other way around.

Balance is key. Don't become the devil in the details rather than the other way around.

Let me tell you a story about Bob, a classic "overthinker" leader. Bob is a highly skilled professional—he's even a black belt in Lean Management, so he knows a thing or two about process improvement. Bob was tasked with leading the implementation of a new project: Transition Care Clinics (TCC). The goal? To reduce hospital readmissions by providing targeted postdischarge care for patients. It was a great initiative with real potential to improve patient outcomes and lower costs for the hospital.

Now Bob, being the meticulous planner that he is, didn't want to leave any stone unturned. So, he did what any Lean Management black belt would do—he started holding meetings. Lots of meetings. Long meetings. Three-hour-long meetings. These sessions would often be filled with introductions, small talk, and then a dictionary full of corporate lingo. I find such lingo quite interesting: "Let's take a deep dive." "Let's get the low-hanging fruit." "Let's circle back." "Let's get in the weeds." "Let's boil the ocean." (Man, so many "let's"!)

Bob's approach wasn't just to outline a basic framework for the clinics—no, he went all in. He created a manual that spanned hundreds of pages, full of complex algorithms, procedural guidelines, and intricate flowcharts for every conceivable scenario.

Now, don't get me wrong—preparation is important, and attention to detail is critical in healthcare. But I hate meetings, especially when they're frequent and long. I believe you can get a lot done in a short amount of time if you focus.

So there we were, stuck in another marathon three-hour meeting, and after hearing everyone introduce themselves for what felt like the hundredth time, I couldn't take it anymore. I looked around the room and saw the fatigue on people's faces.

So, when it was my turn to introduce myself, I decided to change things up. I said, "Hi, I'm Irfan, and I think we can achieve our goals in one hour. What do you all think?"

The room went quiet for a second. You could almost hear the collective sigh of relief as heads nodded around the table. Almost everyone agreed—except for Bob. His face showed clear displeasure. I could see that to him, cutting a three-hour meeting down to one hour was like sacrilege. After all, he had spreadsheets, procedural manuals, and algorithms that needed discussion!

But here's the problem with Bob's approach: While he was hyperfocused on perfecting every detail and analyzing every process, progress slowed to a crawl. He missed the memo on making things simple. Bob's obsession with creating the "perfect" system meant that decisions were delayed and team members felt bogged down by endless meetings. Sure, his manual was impressive—if you wanted a master class in flowcharts and algorithms, Bob had you covered.

But in the meantime, the hospital was still struggling with emergency department patient holds and a constant influx of patients and readmissions, and patients weren't getting the timely care they needed. He actually never asked my opinion or that of others prior to designing the process, and some of us know a thing or two about TCCs.

Months passed, and while Bob continued to refine his masterpiece of a manual, our ED holds were still a mess, and the team was growing frustrated. It wasn't until the hospital administrators started putting pressure on Bob to move forward that the project finally started to pick up speed. But by that point, the rush to implement what had become an overly complex system led to mistakes. Staff members were confused by the layers of procedures, and the very thing Bob had been trying to avoid—chaos—was exactly what ensued.

The lesson here? Sometimes you have to stop analyzing and start acting. Meetings, spreadsheets, and manuals are useful tools, but they can also become distractions. Bob fell into the quagmire of paralysis by analysis, where the fear of making the wrong decision led to endless delays. The truth is, progress doesn't come from perfect plans—it comes from taking action, making adjustments as you go, and learning from the process.

Next time you find yourself stuck in an endless meeting, remember this: You don't need three hours or a hundred-page manual to start making progress. Sometimes all it takes is one hour of focused action. So, whether you're deciding on a new vendor or tackling a huge project, remember that waiting for perfect certainty is a trap. The quagmire of paralysis by analysis will bog you down, keep your team frustrated, and halt progress. The way out? Action. Take a step, learn, adapt, and trust that you'll find your way. Because at the end of the day, leadership isn't about knowing every answer—it's about making things happen.

Practical Steps to Avoid Paralysis by Analysis:

1. **Set a Decision Deadline:** Give yourself (and your team) a reasonable time frame to gather data, but set a hard deadline for making a decision. Don't let it drag on.
2. **Trust Your Gut and Experience:** After doing your research, trust that your knowledge and instincts are enough to move forward. You know more than you think.
3. **Embrace Imperfection:** Accept that no decision will ever be perfect. Some things will go wrong. That's part of the process, and it's how you grow as a leader.
4. **Take the First Step:** Sometimes, the hardest part is just getting started. Take one small action, and you'll often find that momentum builds from there.
5. **Learn as You Go:** Treat decisions as opportunities to learn. If things don't go as planned, adjust and move forward. The key is to keep moving.

FIRE OF IMPULSIVITY

On the opposite end of the spectrum from the quagmire of analysis paralysis, the fire of impulsivity is a leadership trap that burns with immediacy and short-term thinking. It ignites in moments of stress, when quick decisions seem necessary and thoughtful reflection is pushed aside. Leaders who are impulsive often react to situations rather than responding with intentionality. Their knee-jerk decisions, though sometimes effective in the short term, can lead to long-term consequences that derail goals and strategies.

The key to taming impulsivity is patience. Leaders must learn to pause, reflect, and weigh the outcomes before acting. Cultivating emotional intelligence helps to calm the flames of impulsive reactions, allowing decisions to be made from a place of wisdom rather than urgency. The same thing happens at the opposite end of the spectrum when we make decisions too quickly.

We might rush to action based on a set of data, but not stop to ask the critical questions: "How was this data obtained? What's the time frame? What variables were used? Could there be bias involved? Did we connect the dots, or did we just focus on one snapshot of information without seeing the bigger picture?" When we don't take the time to dig deeper, we might miss key insights that could completely change our approach.

And it's not just data. The same thing happens when someone brings a concern or complaint to the leader. Whoever gets to the leader first sometimes wins the "rush-to-judgment" lottery. The leader might make a decision without checking the facts or hearing the other side of the story. You end up making a call based on half truths or assumptions and then realize (a bit too late) that things weren't as they seemed.

I will confess, I've been humbled by these situations more times than I care to admit. I've had to backtrack, correct myself, and own up to mistakes when I didn't follow these principles. And that's okay, because leadership isn't about being perfect. It's about learning to balance thoughtful decision-making with action, knowing when to ask questions and when to trust your gut. It's about embracing imperfection.

BALANCING ANALYSIS AND ACTION

Leadership and sound decision-making are intricately linked. I have observed that the leaders who are the most successful make many small decisions daily and make infrequent big decisions. Their decision-making is not paralyzed by ceaseless data analysis, nor do they need to have 100 percent of the potential information. Sometimes moving fast really does matter.

Great leaders ask their teams to focus the data that will impact a decision and do so without an agenda, ask questions of their team and the data presented, assess the findings as best they are able, and then move quickly into action. This doesn't mean they skimp on gathering information; they just don't get mired in it. And they place what they learn into the larger context of the circumstance and the organization. Too often, leaders don't evaluate the whole continuum before making a decision or are careless enough to not consider the repercussions at every level. Good leaders make informed decisions. And then they communicate them clearly.

When it comes to decision-making, I firmly believe that we often overlook the entire continuum. A decision isn't just about making something happen—it's about understanding how your decision will impact not just one person but all the others involved, their lives, and the interconnected ripple effects it creates. Ultimately, every decision should strive to create balance, even if that balance emerges from another angle or perspective. Without consideration for balance, the result is often a gap or breakdown, something I see happen all too often.

The Chameleon's Mask: Imposter Syndrome

Behind the chameleon's mask I wear lies the familiar trap of imposter syndrome—the crippling feeling that I am a fraud, despite evidence of success. Leaders caught in this trap wear a metaphorical mask, constantly shifting and adjusting to fit the perceived expectations of others. They feel they must blend in, hide their doubts, and conceal their true selves out of fear that they will be exposed as inadequate.

This internalized fear not only undermines one's confidence but also erodes trust within the team. The pressure to maintain a facade often leads to decision paralysis or risk-averse behavior, as leaders may avoid bold choices that could reveal their vulnerabilities. To remove the mask, leaders must embrace vulnerability, trust in their abilities, and recognize that everyone—no matter how accomplished—faces moments of doubt.

Vulnerability is often misunderstood. Many people equate it with weakness, thinking that revealing their true selves or exposing their flaws makes them fragile. But the reality couldn't be further from the truth. Vulnerability in its purest form is an incredible source of strength—it's the foundation for building genuine connections, fostering trust, and developing authentic leadership.

To be vulnerable is to be real, to be human, and that's where true relationships are formed. If you're constantly putting up a front or projecting an image that you think people want to see, those around you may never truly trust you. Why? Because they sense the facade.

And how can you expect to build real, meaningful connections with others when you're hiding behind a wall of perceived perfection?

Effective leaders understand the significance of their track record, recognizing that it reflects their actions, decisions, and overall performance over time. This acknowledgment is rooted in the understanding that trust and credibility are earned through consistent and transparent behavior. Leaders who genuinely care about their track record are aware that short-term deception may momentarily sway perceptions but that sustained trust requires authenticity and reliability. One can fool someone for a day, a month, or a year, but eventually people figure it out. Authenticity is at the root of leadership integrity.

Vulnerability in its purest form is an incredible source of strength—it's the foundation for building genuine connections, fostering trust, and developing authentic leadership.

Even as I write this book, I can't ignore my discomfort. It's not easy to share some of the private thoughts or moments of vulnerability that have shaped me. There's always that voice in the back of my mind asking, *What will people think of me?* There's a certain level of exposure that comes with sharing personal stories, and the truth is, it's uncomfortable. But let's be clear: exposing vulnerability is not about confession or disclosing every regret or airing dirty laundry; it's about learning through experience, sharing the lessons that come from vulnerability, and being honest with yourself and others.

In fact, like I said before, I still introduce myself as a "fake CEO." Part of it comes from my discomfort with titles. I've never really liked them. Titles have a way of making things sound official, hierarchical, and—frankly—unreal. The other part is this little voice inside me that wonders if people will really believe it. After all, it sometimes still feels strange that I'm in this position—the immigrant who used to clean carpets is now sitting in boardrooms leading discussions on healthcare and leadership. It's a surreal thought that doesn't always feel like it fits. But in that discomfort I have learned to excel, and this is exactly where I've learned the value of vulnerability.

I still remember the first time I was asked to present "my story" to hospital boards across the state. I was surprised, to say the least. Why would they want to hear my story? What could I offer to rooms full of seasoned experts in healthcare? I wasn't a conventional speaker, and I certainly didn't have a polished narrative like the ones you see in leadership seminars. But they asked, and I said yes.

I prepared the slides, practiced what I was going to say, and then awkwardly walked into rooms filled with hundreds of people—all eyes on me, waiting to hear my story. I was nervous every single time. I thought to myself, *Is this going to be the start of a really good joke?* Picture this: an immigrant Pakistani carpet cleaner walks into a room full of healthcare experts at one of the largest health systems in the United States to talk about leadership skills …

The irony wasn't lost on me, but I walked into those halls every time, stood behind the podium, and shared my story. Not a polished, perfect, corporate version—but the real story. My story. And guess what? People listened. They connected. Not because my journey was flawless but because it was real. It was filled with vulnerability, uncomfortable truths, and moments I wasn't necessarily proud of. And that's precisely why it resonated.

Vulnerability is what breaks down barriers between people. It shows you're not just another person with a rehearsed success story—you're a human being who has made mistakes, learned from them, and grown. And in leadership, that's what matters most. People don't want to follow someone who pretends to be perfect. They want to follow someone who is authentic, someone who can admit when they don't have all the answers, and someone they can trust.

When you show vulnerability, it gives others permission to do the same. It creates a culture where people can be themselves, speak up when they're unsure, and admit when they need help. In doing so, you foster trust—one of the most critical components of any team. Without trust, people hold back, afraid to speak their minds or take risks. But when trust is present, real collaboration can happen. Ideas flow freely, innovation occurs, and people work better together.

Vulnerability isn't a weakness—it's a leadership superpower. It's about being brave enough to be seen for who you truly are and to let others do the same. It's acknowledging that you're still learning, still evolving, and open to growth. That's what real leadership is. Not projecting an image of perfection but leading by example through honesty and transparency.

The next time you're afraid to share your story or are holding back, fearing what others might think, remember this: True connection happens when you're real. People don't want the fake version of you—they want the human version. And when you lead with vulnerability, you give people the opportunity to connect with the real you, to trust you, and to follow you.

The truth is, writing this book and sharing my journey is uncomfortable. It requires me to be vulnerable in a very public way. But if someone takes the time to read it and finds even a single lesson in these words, then it's worth it. Vulnerability builds bridges. It creates the space for growth, both for you and for those around you. That's the kind of leader I want to be—the one who isn't afraid to show up fully, flaws and all. Because that's how you inspire others to do the same.

Quicksand of Ego and Illusion of Control

"Don't get so big that when you look for heaven, you look down." I'm paraphrasing, but the gist of this saying is often attributed to Maya Angelou. That's what ego does to you. Better, as Angelou knew, to look down on someone only if you are in the act of helping them up.

Egotistical leaders, like "Dr. Smith," get trapped by their ego. It is important to be confident, yet if unchecked, ego can lead to disaster. Egotistical leaders get bogged down by micromanagement, they are resistant to feedback, they don't accept accountability, and they lack empathy. My advice is this: If one cannot check one's ego, then one must at least try to camouflage it.

Ego is often the by-product of our insecurities—a constant battle within ourselves to win and maintain dominance. While a healthy level of confidence can propel us forward, unchecked ego leads us down a destructive path. It fosters jealousy, clouds our judgment, and results in bad decisions. Worse yet, it can create a poisonous culture where collaboration is replaced by competition and genuine connection is overshadowed by the need to outshine others. Burning to win and compare. There will always be someone younger than you, someone smarter than you, someone more educated than you, someone more accomplished than you, someone richer than you ... there is no end. The only real competition is with yourself. You should never lose the desire to get better.

In environments dominated by a leader's ego, people feel threatened rather than inspired. Instead of building each other up, the focus shifts to tearing others down, perpetuating a cycle of negativity. This not only harms individual growth but also prevents teams from achieving their collective potential. Ultimately, a culture driven by ego is one where trust erodes, creativity suffers, and true leadership is lost.

THE CURSE OF SELF-DECEPTION

Self-deception is as problematic as outward deception. Leaders who overcommit or are too optimistic create patterns of failure. These are products of ego. I fell into the trap of overcommitting myself. Juggling multiple projects and responsibilities led to burnout and compromised the quality of my work. I learned the importance of setting realistic priorities and delegating tasks to maintain a healthy work-life balance. On the other hand, while optimism is generally positive, I learned that excessive optimism without a realistic assessment of challenges can lead to unpreparedness. Balancing optimism with a pragmatic understanding of potential obstacles is crucial for effective leadership.

How often have I found myself on a thin beam that seemed suspended over hot lava? In the past, particularly in the first years running the first healthcare organization I formed, I was guilty of micromanagement. Wanting to ensure everything was done perfectly, I excessively controlled tasks and stifled creativity within the team. It took feedback from team members for me to realize the importance of empowering others and trusting their capabilities. I learned that it is okay for others to fail—just as I had multiple times—because they will learn. People need to be guided, not controlled.

I recall an incident from nearly a decade ago that still echoes in my memory. A new hospital CEO ventured into the physician's lounge. Following a brief introduction to those gathered, he embarked on a self-assured narrative, recounting how he had successfully captured his previous market before coming to this one and how he ultimately aimed to dominate hospital-based healthcare for the entire area. I found myself struck by his audacious ego and, more notably, his apparent obliviousness to the implications of his words and the audience before him.

The lounge, a space where collaboration and cooperation among physicians should have been the focal point, transformed into a stage for a display of unchecked power trips. The CEO's inability to gauge the room and comprehend the potential repercussions of his words proved to be a critical misstep. Little did he realize that among the attentive audience sat individuals directly impacted by his past actions and others potentially threatened by his future ambitions.

The consequences of this ill-timed revelation rippled through the hospital and beyond. The seeds of discord were sown as trust eroded, and concerns about the CEO's intentions permeated the area medical community. His boastful narrative not only strained relationships within the hospital but sparked apprehension and dissent among physicians and staff, who now questioned the leadership's ethical compass. In the end, the CEO's journey took an unexpected turn. His grandiose ego, showcased in that fateful encounter, ultimately became the catalyst for the unraveling of his career. The lack of humility and foresight that characterized his leadership style led to internal strife, external scrutiny, and, ultimately, his departure from the helm.

This tale signifies the value of vigilance and serves as a cautionary reminder that leadership is not merely about accomplishments and market dominance. It is equally about understanding the nuances of human interactions, recognizing the impact of words, and fostering an environment of trust and collaboration. I often say that I never forget the human factor in business and medicine.

The Abyss of Black-and-White Thinking

Now, let me share a bit of personal hypocrisy. I'm not exactly a fan of gray—like, literally. My closet is pretty black and white. But when it comes to decision-making, the world is all shades of gray. I have already talked at length about the philosophy of shades of gray—a concept I've come to appreciate more and more over the years. The truth is that life—and leadership especially—is rarely black and white. It's one of the most important lessons I've learned. But for now, let's chat about the opposite of that—the dangerous abyss of thinking in black and white, a dangerous oversimplification of reality. In this trap, leaders see things in binary terms: success or failure, right or wrong, strong or weak.

Let me introduce you to this guy—you probably know someone like him. He's a leader who thrives in complexity, making bold decisions and solving tough problems, yet most mornings he can't find his keys or wallet. His life is a mix of sharp competence and everyday chaos, from managing high-stakes situations to hunting through couch cushions.

What sets him apart is his comfort with ambiguity. He sees life in shades of gray, takes risks on unconventional ideas, and navigates the messy middle where others get stuck. That balance of creativity and practicality is what makes him successful. Oh, and that guy? He's me.

I'm the guy who constantly loses his keys and wallet and even forgets where he parked. It drives my wife—and me—nuts, despite her heroic efforts to keep my chaos in check. My mom once told me, "If you just put things where they belong, you'd be successful." She wasn't wrong.

But I've come to accept that organizing my closet isn't my strength, though I try—big-picture thinking maybe is. While I may not excel at keeping track of some details, I thrive in complexity, solving nuanced problems and taking risks others might avoid. I don't see the world in black and white; I find opportunity in the gray areas, where innovation happens and growth occurs.

You don't have to be perfect to succeed. Life is about balance, flexibility, and leaning into what you're good at, even if it means needing trackers for your keys. So no, I'll continue to work on my opportunities. I'm okay with that. Being a good leader—or trying to be a better person—isn't about perfection; it's about adapting, trusting, and making the most of your strengths. Just don't ask me to find my keys—and yes, thank you, I do have air tags.

MEET PEOPLE IN THE MIDDLE

Sometimes you have to bet on people who don't check all the boxes. Maybe they didn't go to the best schools or have the perfect qualifications, but something tells you they've got potential. Or take companies, for example. Sure, it's easy to put all your trust in the big, national firms that are well known and have fancy logos. But sometimes the right answer is partnering with a local company that doesn't have national recognition but has the heart, hustle, and the right connections to get things done.

It's the same with leadership. You have to meet people in the middle—not everything is a battle in which you win or lose. Sometimes it's about finding a compromise, a shade of gray, where both sides get a little bit of what they need. You don't have to get 100 percent all the time. That's where the magic happens.

> Not everything is a battle in which you win or lose. Sometimes it's about finding a compromise.

Let's look at leadership like a poker game. You don't always get a winning hand. Sometimes you're betting on a person who doesn't have the best hand—or at least doesn't look like it on paper. Maybe they're the one who didn't graduate from an Ivy League school or doesn't have a glittering résumé. But they show up with passion and grit, and when the chips are down, they're the one who surprises you by going all in and winning the pot.

Now, black-and-white thinkers? They would fold those cards every time. They'd see the stats, the so-called facts, and dismiss the potential hidden in the gray areas. But here's the thing—you don't win big by playing it safe all the time. You've got to take risks, sometimes on people who don't fit the perfect mold. Sometimes you just gamble.

The abyss of black-and-white thinking is seductive. It feels safe to categorize everything as good or bad, right or wrong. But leadership—and life—is so much more complex than that. The magic happens when you learn to embrace the gray areas. When you can take a step back and see that not every decision has to be perfect. Sometimes you have to choose the best option in front of you, even if it's not ideal. Sometimes you have to bet on people, even if they don't fit the traditional mold. And sometimes you just have to accept that you won't find your keys until your wife comes to the rescue.

So, if you catch yourself falling into that trap of thinking everything is black or white, remind yourself of the power of gray. It's where opportunities live, where flexibility is found, and where real connections are made. Life is messy. Leadership is messy. But when you get comfortable with the discomfort of not having all the answers, when you can see beyond the stark lines of black and white, that's when you start making the best decisions—ones that are full of heart, humanity, and sometimes even a little humor.

And who knows? Maybe one day you'll find your keys without needing help.

Flow like Water; Embrace Change

One of my favorite statements is "we will figure this out." Perhaps the most vital lesson in leadership is to "flow like water"—to embrace change with grace and adaptability. Water, by its very nature, does not resist obstacles; it moves, shifts, and transforms according to its environment. It can be calm and still, or it can rage in torrents, carving new paths. It even evaporates to rain somewhere else or transforms itself to ice, hard as rock. The leader who embraces the qualities of water learns to navigate the inevitable shifts of circumstances with fluidity, finding strength in flexibility rather than rigidity.

If ego can be a surefire fast track to downfall, so can the inability to be nimble. Nimbleness, or agility, refers to the ability to adapt quickly and effectively to new circumstances, challenges, and diverse environments. Being nimble in leadership is crucial for navigating the dynamic and ever-changing landscape of the modern world. Leaders who are not nimble, who are not able to pivot dynamically when facing changing situations or new people, eventually fail.

Unlike the traps we discussed earlier—perfectionism, ego, impulsivity, or overanalysis—leaders who flow like water are neither overly controlling nor passive. Instead, they are adaptive. They understand that clinging to a fixed plan or resisting change can be a path to stagnation. Water finds a way through, around or over any obstacle it encounters while maintaining its essence. This is how leaders must be: willing to adjust course without losing sight of their ultimate vision.

Imagine a river flowing steadily down a mountainside. The river has a clear destination: the valley below. Along the way, rocks, trees, and sudden drops create obstacles. But water doesn't stop in frustration or try to resist these barriers. Instead, it adapts. When faced with a boulder, water finds a way around it, reshaping its path while still moving forward. When it encounters a steep fall, it cascades with even more energy, embracing the drop as an opportunity to gather momentum. In some places, the river slows and spreads, giving life to the ecosystem around it; in others, it narrows and rushes, using its power to carve through solid rock.

For a leader, this metaphor illustrates the importance of adaptability. When an unexpected crisis hits—a sudden market shift, a loss of resources, or internal conflict—leaders who "flow like water" don't panic or resist. Instead, they assess the situation, adjust their strategies, and keep moving forward. They know that every challenge is an opportunity to grow and evolve, just as the river becomes more defined and powerful by overcoming the obstacles in its path.

The story of COVID-19 is one that no one could have predicted, and it's a perfect example of adaptability and agility in action. When the pandemic hit, we were thrown into an unknown, overwhelming situation. We faced an epidemic without truly understanding how it spread, how it affected the body, or how long it would last. Suddenly, everything we knew—personally, professionally, and clinically—was thrown out the window. We had to learn how to survive, adapt, and lead in a world turned upside down. My colleagues and I were responsible for caring for thousands of patients, and my wife was responsible for vaccinating forty thousand people. Yet neither of us knew what we were dealing with at the outset of the pandemic.

In those early days, it felt like a daily battle just to keep up. We had to figure out how to protect our patients, ourselves, and our families from a virus that seemed to change its nature every day. Should we disinfect everything? Should we wear masks? Inject Lysol? Take antimalarial? The stakes were high. It wasn't just about managing tasks—it was about keeping people safe, providing clear direction when we barely had any ourselves, and making decisions with incomplete information.

Overnight, businesses had to pivot—yes, pivot ... I said it—to remote work. And allow me to say, I don't know how many times I heard the word *pivot* in those endless meetings. If I had a nickel for every time someone said *pivot*, I might have made a small fortune. But that's exactly what we had to do. Everything changed, and we had to adapt fast. The way we worked, communicated, and led was redefined in real time. In my case, most of us were in the hospital, to continue showing up on the front lines.

Everyone was doing their best just to keep the wheels turning. Hospitals were flooded with patients. Physicians, nurses, and staff worked long hours, often at great personal risk, with limited knowledge about how to treat a virus that was spreading like wildfire. Sacrifices were made daily as medical professionals went above and beyond to save lives while trying to keep themselves and their families safe.

It even took a personal toll at times, when my wife would start a meeting at 3:30 a.m. or start driving at 4:00 a.m. to vaccinate people at distant camps while I was trying to run the groups and at the same time homeschool kids.

But over time, we learned to survive and adapt. We learned how to protect ourselves better. We figured out how to live and work with a virus that had upended our world. Clinically, we developed better treatments, learned how to manage care, and eventually vaccines brought hope back into the picture. Businesses found new ways to operate—whether through technology or by finding creative ways to meet their customers' needs in the midst of chaos.

We learned how to pivot (there's that word again), but more importantly, we learned how to lead through uncertainty, how to sacrifice for the greater good, and how to adapt to survive and succeed. In the end, COVID-19 reminded us that leadership isn't about having the perfect plan; it's about adapting to the world as it is, making sacrifices where necessary, and continuing to move forward even when the path is unclear. And yes, it's about pivoting—again and again—until we find our way through.

It all comes down to resilience, adaptability, patience, and letting go of control. Water is resilient and persistent. It doesn't give up when faced with an obstacle, nor does it remain stagnant. As a leader, resilience is about pushing forward despite setbacks while remaining open to new possibilities. Agility, adaptability—these traits in a leader ensure that when failure arrives, it will be failure that instructs, providing another opportunity for flexible, resilient thinking to find a new way forward. Water always finds its way.

Flow like Water: A Mindset

- **Adaptability**: Just as water changes its form–becoming a solid, liquid, or gas–leaders must be adaptable to shifting environments. A rigid mindset, like a dam holding back water, will eventually crack under pressure. Flexibility allows leaders to meet change with creativity.
- **Power in Patience**: Water can be both gentle and powerful. Over time, a steady drip can carve through stone. Leaders who understand the power of patience can steadily work toward their goals, adapting to obstacles without losing their core values or purpose.
- **Letting Go of Control**: Water moves where it needs to, unconcerned with forcing its way in any single direction. A leader who lets go of the illusion of control empowers their team and adapts to shifting conditions, knowing that leadership is not about micromanaging every detail but about guiding the overall flow.

The Bridge of Clarity: Leadership Communication

A good leader is a good communicator. Without the ability to communicate, we can never collaborate. Absent effective communication, some leaders struggle to foster a work environment where individuals feel comfortable sharing their ideas. It's important to recognize that ideas often originate from a collaborative process. Throughout history, significant ideas and accomplishments have typically been the result of contributions from many individuals. When these diverse ideas come together, the collective result can be towering and impactful.

Ideas rarely strike like a singular bolt of lightning; rather, they resemble various pieces of wood rubbing together to ignite a fire. Or, to change analogies, consider one of my favorites: the way an orchestra is formed of individuals each playing a different part of the score and each expert at different musical instruments; when violin, cello, drums, trumpets come together, it results in the creation of a beautiful symphony. Listening to other ideas leads to innovation and success.

Someone once said to me that it is important that you walk toward your own dreams, otherwise you will end up working for someone else's. I'm a believer that people find it more valuable if you can meet others at a midpoint where you can build a dream together, and when it is a shared vision, its shared success results in mutual benefit and a greater pride. Real collaboration, and with it real self-directed accountability, allows teams to make beautiful music together. When listening to Mozart, no one really cares who is first chair, second chair, conductor; in the end, their positions don't mean anything—roles do.

Where do we start? The most important task in communication is to confirm that your message was understood. It's too easy to assume that people "get you." And too costly when they don't. Many times

I have felt that I'd conveyed what I meant, but I didn't realize that it was never understood. There were instances when I assumed that communication was clear without confirming understanding from the team. This resulted in misunderstandings and errors. I now prioritize clear and transparent communication, ensuring that key messages are conveyed effectively.

One of the other most essential skills a good leader can develop is the ability to have critical conversations—those difficult, often uncomfortable discussions where opinions clash, stakes are high, and priorities differ. These conversations, when handled with care, can lead to clarity, better decision-making, and stronger relationships. But when handled poorly, they can lead to broken trust, damaged relationships, and fractured teams.

Here's the thing: Leaders must communicate clearly without severing ties, especially when navigating disagreements. You don't need everyone to always agree with you; in fact, a diversity of perspectives is what often makes teams successful. But the ability to disagree productively, without letting emotions take control or damaging the relationship, is what distinguishes a strong leader from a reactive one.

Here's another skill: It's essential to remember that how you show up matters just as much as what you say. Effective communication isn't just about the words you use. It's about how you present—your tone, your body language, your pauses, and the way you listen. Every interaction becomes a bridge to either clarity or confusion.

How We Communicate Matters

Leadership communication happens in many forms—verbally, nonverbally, and in writing. Each one plays a crucial role in how we're perceived and, more importantly, how our messages are received.

- **Emails and Texts—the Written Word:** As a rule, I never email or text anything that I don't want to be forwarded. Now, let's start with the fundamentals, the way we write emails and texts. The written word is powerful, but it's also easily misunderstood. When you write an email or a text, you lose tone and nonverbal cues that people rely on for understanding intent. A quick message, if poorly worded, can come off as cold or dismissive when you meant it to be clear and straightforward.

  When writing, ask yourself this: ***Am I being clear without being harsh or insulting? Am I addressing the core issue, or am I letting my emotions dictate the tone?*** Taking a moment to pause before hitting Send allows you to consider how your message will land. Sometimes that pause gives you the perspective needed to soften an unnecessarily sharp point or to clarify a vague instruction.

- **Verbal Communication—What We Say Is Important; How We Say It Is More Important:** When you speak, do you allow yourself time to pause, or do you fill every moment with words? Often, in critical conversations, people are uncomfortable with pauses and tend to give rushed, emotional responses. Pausing allows you to think before you speak. It shows that you're being thoughtful and intentional in your response. It creates room for reflection—for both you and the person you're speaking with. Just consider what Debussy said: "Music is the space between notes," otherwise it would be just noise.

- **Nonverbal Communication–What We Don't Say Is Often as Important as What We Do**: Your body language, facial expressions, and gestures can either open up a conversation, or your face can have closed captioning. Turn it off; shut it down. If you're crossing your arms or avoiding eye contact, the person on the other side of the conversation may feel like you're closed off to their perspective, even if your words suggest otherwise.

  Nonverbal communication is about showing engagement. Are you leaning in to listen? Are you nodding in understanding, even if you don't agree? These subtle cues can make the other person feel heard and valued, which is crucial when opinions differ. A leader who masters nonverbal communication can manage disagreements without escalating tensions.

- **The Power of Listening:** Listening is arguably the most important communication skill in a communication. It's not just about hearing words; it's about understanding what's behind those words. People want to feel that their ideas are valued, even if their ideas don't align with yours. When leaders truly listen, it signals respect and openness. This doesn't mean you have to agree, but it shows that you're considering their point of view before responding. It also gives you a moment to compose a thoughtful response. This helps you avoid knee-jerk reactions that can damage relationships.

BUILDING BRIDGES TO CLARITY THROUGH COMMUNICATION

To communicate effectively as a leader, you have to consider how you're building bridges with every interaction. Whether it's a quick email, a team meeting, or a one-on-one conversation, each moment is an opportunity to strengthen or weaken the relationship. Clarity in communication doesn't mean saying the most—it means saying the right thing, at the right time, in the right way.

When we master the art of having critical conversations—whether through verbal communication, emails, or even the unspoken language of our body—we create an environment where different opinions are welcomed, high priorities are managed with respect, and disagreements are opportunities for growth rather than division.

In the end, a leader's ability to communicate thoughtfully is what transforms difficult conversations into productive ones. It's how you maintain the balance between assertiveness and empathy and how you ensure that even in the face of differing opinions, the bridges to clarity remain intact.

Mixing transparency at times with diplomacy in communication is a high art. It's not deception; it's knowing where you can't compromise on personal, professional, and fiduciary responsibilities.

Mixing transparency at times with diplomacy in communication is a high art. It's not deception; it's knowing where you can't compromise on personal, professional, and fiduciary responsibilities. Not all possess it. My friend, let's call him Mike, had a unique talent for dropping truth bombs that could leave a room in stunned silence. The guy had no filter. It was as if there was a direct line from his brain to his mouth, bypassing any semblance of tact. Sadly, because of his lack of filter, most people missed out on who he truly was. He was truly a great guy with a big heart and not a single evil bone in his body, but his mind was wired differently than most.

So one day, after yet another cringeworthy comment, I decided I couldn't take it anymore. I strolled into a bookstore and picked up a gem titled *Emotional Intelligence*, by Daniel Goldman. It is like the bible for understanding others' feelings and social cues. I thought, *Maybe Mike could use a dose of this wisdom.*

I waltzed up to him, book in hand, and with a poker face that could rival a professional card player, I said, "Hey, I stumbled upon this book recently, and I loved it. Seriously, take a look."

He glanced at the title and shot back, "Why would I need this book?" I couldn't help but chuckle.

I looked at him and said, "Well, my friend, that right there is exactly why you need it." Whenever someone tells me that they are a "straight shooter," I cringe!

Mastering the Basement—the Power of Self-Control

The primitive part of the brain, namely the amygdala and the medulla oblongata, plays a vital role in managing instinctual reactions to threats, forming the foundation of the fight-or-flight response. The amygdala acts as a sentinel, detecting danger and triggering emotional responses such as fear or aggression. Meanwhile, the medulla oblongata, part of the brain stem, or "basement," as I call it, controls involuntary functions like heart rate and breathing, ensuring that the body is physically primed to act in moments of perceived danger.

According to an article in *Harvard Health Publishing* titled "Understanding the Stress Response," this system evolved to protect early humans from life-threatening predators, but today it can be activated by nonlethal stressors like work pressure or relationship conflicts.[26] Recognizing how the amygdala and medulla oblongata

26 "Understanding the Stress Response: Chronic Activation of This Survival Mechanism Impairs Health," *Harvard Health Publishing*, April 3, 2024, https://www.health.harvard.edu/staying-healthy/understanding-the-stress-response.

(basement) influence our reactions can help us better manage stress and improve emotional regulation.

In moments of conflict or high stress, it's crucial to recognize when you're operating from the basement. In leadership, especially in challenging environments like healthcare, your response to hostility or pressure can either strengthen relationships or irreparably damage them.

When you're "in the basement," you're stuck in survival mode—ready to fight, freeze, or flee. These reactions are automatic and can be helpful in moments of real physical danger, but in the context of professional interactions, they can lead to impulsive decisions, rash words, and regrettable actions. A single emotionally charged email, text, or verbal response can fracture trust, damage your reputation, and even end important relationships.

I know I could do better in this department. It is a struggle at times, both personally and professionally. However, as I try to better myself, I try to remember that it's essential to recognize when we're feeling cornered or defensive and to pause before reacting. In these moments, our brains are not fully engaged in rational thinking—we're simply trying to survive the perceived threat. That's why self-control begins with self-awareness. When you feel your heart race or your emotions spike, take a moment to check whether you're in the basement of your brain.

Instead of firing off a quick, heated response, stop and take a deep breath. Sometimes just a deep breath can interrupt the fight-or-flight mechanism and give you the clarity needed to respond thoughtfully. Or better yet, give yourself permission to sleep on it. Some of my colleagues are well aware of my statement "well, let's sleep on it." Emotions tend to settle after a bit of time, allowing your rational mind to regain control. You'll often find that what seemed urgent or enraging in the moment looks entirely different after a break.

When you pause, breathe, and allow your emotional state to calm down, you regain access to the higher-thinking parts of your brain—the prefrontal cortex—where logic, empathy, and sound decision-making reside. It's in this state that you can evaluate your response, consider the long-term consequences, and choose to either reply carefully or, sometimes, not reply at all.

By mastering the art of taking a moment before you respond, you not only avoid saying something you'll regret but also strengthen your ability to lead with grace, build trust, and maintain strong, positive relationships. Self-control isn't about suppressing emotion—it's about learning to manage it and respond from a place of wisdom rather than impulse.

> Self-control isn't about suppressing emotion–it's about learning to manage it and respond from a place of wisdom rather than impulse.

I recall many times when I practiced pausing for a bit in certain situations where I could have said certain things that would have gotten me into trouble and other times things I said where I put my foot in my mouth.

"Disagreements don't make enemies; it's how we handle them that defines the relationships we build."[27]

Avoiding the Traps

Leadership is full of challenges, but some of the most dangerous pitfalls are the ones we unknowingly create for ourselves. The traps of leadership—whether it's paralysis by analysis, ego-driven decisions, or black-and-white thinking—can derail even the most well-intentioned leader.

---

27 Bill Walsh, *The Score Takes Care of Itself* (Portfolio Publishing, 2010).

Recognizing these traps is the first step toward avoiding them, but what separates truly great leaders from the rest is their ability to navigate around these obstacles with self-awareness, adaptability, and a commitment to growth.

Leadership isn't about perfection, and it's certainly not about having all the answers. It's about being aware of your blind spots, understanding that vulnerability is strength, and knowing when to pause, reflect, and course correct. In the face of complexity, a good leader doesn't get lost in the details or overwhelmed by the enormity of the task at hand. Instead, they find a way to move forward, making decisions that are thoughtful, balanced, and focused on the greater good.

Avoiding these leadership traps also means building genuine connections—by communicating clearly, listening deeply, and leading with empathy. Critical conversations are not to be feared but embraced as opportunities for clarity and growth. Trust, after all, is built not just on agreement but on how we handle disagreements and manage priorities without breaking relationships.

In the end, leadership is not about the title or the power it affords—it's about the sacrifices you make, the bridges you build, and the legacy you leave. The journey is filled with difficult decisions and potential missteps, but by staying conscious of these traps, you can lead with confidence, clarity, and authenticity. Leadership is about progress, not perfection—and navigating these traps with grace is what makes that progress possible.

DYNAMIC DANCE

This painting combines the vibrancy of cubism with the classical richness of Renaissance color palettes, depicting two figures in motion against a fragmented geometric background. The figures—a woman on the left and a man on the right—are rendered in angular, stylized forms. Their gestures suggest a dance, symbolizing a dynamic interaction between contrasting elements, possibly East and West.

CHAPTER 12

Relationships: Human Bonds, Broken and Forged

A relationship is like a dance—sometimes you lead, sometimes you follow, and sometimes you need to sit back and let the music guide you both.
—UNKNOWN

The question of what it means to be human and the significance of our journey in creating relationships touches on some of the most profound aspects of our existence. Our interactions with each other, whether in pairs, groups, villages, tribes, or in the complex civilizations we have formed, create bonds of interdependence. At its core, being human means being capable of creation, connection, and imagination. These abilities have allowed us to shape our environments, build complex societies, and even define who we are collectively and individually.

As Yuval Noah Harari writes in *Sapiens: A Brief History of Humankind*, "We have mastered our surroundings, increased food production, built cities, established empires and created far-flung trade networks. But did we decrease the amount of suffering in the world?"[28]

In other words, are we happy?

Human relationships are unique because they are not just about survival or procreation; they are about connection, understanding, and shared meaning. We build bonds that evolve, grow, and sometimes break, and we are shaped by them in profound ways. It's this complexity—the emotional depth, the empathy, the cultural significance, and the spiritual resonance—that makes human relationships unlike any other. They define us as individuals and as a species. They define what it means to be human.

Love, adoration, and acceptance—not to be confused with tolerance—form the foundation of any meaningful relationship. Tolerance implies putting up with something that irritates or challenges us, a sort of resigned endurance. Acceptance, however, is different. It means embracing the other person as they are, without condition or need for change. Acceptance allows relationships to deepen, bringing a level of authenticity and openness that tolerance alone can't achieve.

Another crucial aspect of relationships, often overlooked, is gratitude. In the routines and familiarity that inevitably set in over time, we sometimes forget to appreciate the people closest to us. Gratitude acts as a quiet, steady anchor, reminding us to recognize the gifts others bring to our lives—whether that's a partner's steady presence, a friend's understanding,

Gratitude acts as a quiet, steady anchor, reminding us to recognize the gifts others bring to our lives—whether that's a partner's steady presence, a friend's understanding, or a family member's unconditional love.

28 Yuval Noah Harari, *Sapiens: A Brief History of Humankind* (New York: Harper, 2015).

or a family member's unconditional love. When we express gratitude, we keep the connection alive, reminding both ourselves and the other person of the value they add to our lives.

Gratitude transforms relationships. It shifts our focus from what we lack or what irritates us to what we cherish. It encourages us to see each other through a lens of appreciation rather than expectation. In this way, gratitude becomes the soil in which love, adoration, and acceptance can continue to grow, deepening our bonds and bringing warmth and resilience to our relationships

We often fall off the wagon; indeed, I do too. Sometimes we need to be reminded—something my wife has become an expert at doing. Other times, self-reflection is enough to get us back on board.

Love is not just a feeling; it is also a form of creative expression. Just like a painter approaches a blank canvas, we approach each relationship as a blank space where we can cocreate something beautiful. The relationship becomes a joint creative expression, evolving through shared experiences, joys, and challenges.

Love is not just a feeling; it is also a form of creative expression. Just like a painter approaches a blank canvas, we approach each relationship as a blank space where we can cocreate something beautiful. The relationship becomes a joint creative expression, evolving through shared experiences, joys, and challenges.

Instead of viewing relationships in terms of success or failure, we can see each relationship as our teacher. Every connection we have—whether it lasts a month or a lifetime—teaches us something about ourselves, about others, or about the world. This approach makes it easier to let go when necessary and to appreciate every relationship for the growth it offers.

Capacity for Connection

An essential part of being human is our capacity for connection. We are social beings, and our survival has always depended on our ability to bond, cooperate, and build trust within groups. In early human history, we formed small, tight-knit communities—villages and tribes—where everyone knew each other and shared the burdens and benefits of daily life. Over time, these groups grew larger and more complex, leading to cities and societies bound by shared culture, language, laws, and goals.

This scaling up of human connection, from family units to sprawling metropolises, shows an amazing flexibility in our social structures. We're capable of creating shared identities and values with people we might never meet personally, which enables the formation of nations, cultures, and even global communities. These social connections give us a sense of belonging and purpose, reminding us that our lives are part of something larger than ourselves.

Our ability to imagine, to build, and to connect with one another has allowed us to create cultures, societies, and civilizations that are as fragile as they are resilient. And as we continue to evolve, both socially and technologically, these same abilities will guide us. We are storytellers and builders, bound together by shared dreams and shared struggles. And this, ultimately, may be the most human thing of all: the knowledge that, despite our individual differences, we are all part of the same journey, crafting the story of who we are and who we might become.

Just as with financial investments, relationships require careful attention, effort, and growth over time. We wouldn't expect a stagnant investment portfolio to flourish, and the same holds true for the bonds we share with others and ourselves. A healthy life is one where relationships are constantly nurtured, diversified, and reassessed. Some relationships grow stronger with time, while others require adjustment or even letting go. Regardless of the type, each relationship adds a layer of richness to our experience, expanding our capacity for love, empathy, and understanding.

In the same way a savvy investor diversifies their financial assets to balance risk and reward, we too must continue to invest in relationships. Personal relationships, friendships, familial bonds, professional connections, and the relationship we have with ourselves—all serve different yet essential roles in our lives. Just as we wouldn't pour all our money into a single stock, it is important to invest our emotional energy judiciously into each and different facets of our relationships. The different types of relationships we cultivate offer unique forms of support, joy, and learning, creating a more balanced and fulfilling life.

However, it's not enough to simply form these connections. Relationships, like investments, must grow over time. They require consistent attention—small, everyday acts of care, communication, and understanding. Neglect them, and even the most promising bonds can weaken. But when we make the effort to invest in our relationships, we see returns far greater than any material wealth: deeper connections, a sense of belonging, and emotional resilience.

To live fully is to engage actively in this ongoing process of investment. Whether through moments of joy, conflict, or quiet companionship, our relationships shape who we are and who we can become. The more we invest in them—by being present, open, and willing to grow—the richer our lives will be, not just for ourselves but for everyone we connect with. Each type of relationship we participate in plays a unique role in individuals' lives and contributes to their social and emotional well-being.

Cultivating a Better Relationship with Yourself

One relationship we often neglect to speak of is the relationship with the self. It starts with self-reflection and understanding your own identity. Being human means being able to reflect on ourselves and question our purpose. We don't just live; we seek meaning in our lives. This is why humans have developed philosophy, religion, science, and art—these are all ways of grappling with the fundamental questions of existence. Who are we? Why are we here? What should we strive for? This quest for self-understanding and purpose is uniquely human, and it continues to shape us, individually and collectively.

We often focus on our relationships with others—our friends, partners, family—but the relationship we nurture with ourselves is perhaps the most significant one we'll ever have. Like any other relationship, it requires time, care, and intentional effort. Developing a deeper, more compassionate connection with yourself isn't just a path to personal fulfillment; it's essential for fostering healthier relationships with others too. But how do you build a meaningful relationship with yourself?

This isn't simply knowing your likes and dislikes but truly understanding who you are beneath the surface. It's about peeling back the layers of external validation, societal expectations, and past conditioning to discover your authentic self. At the same time, it is essential to understand your blind spots, and how you react to those things that set you off provides you with a deeper insight.

The foundation of a healthy relationship with yourself begins with self-awareness. Ask yourself the following:

- What motivates me?
- What are my core values?
- What do I need to feel safe, loved, and fulfilled?

It is a mental exercise we don't do enough. These questions invite introspection and encourage you to listen deeply. Practicing mindfulness or journaling can aid in this process, giving you a space to reflect on your experiences, emotions, and personal growth. Being aware of your strengths and limitations helps you approach life with clarity and intention.

Just as we offer empathy to those we love, self-compassion calls for extending that same kindness inward. Often we are our own harshest critics, quick to judge ourselves for perceived failures or shortcomings. But developing a better relationship with yourself means learning to respond to your imperfections with understanding rather than criticism.

Embrace the practice of treating yourself as you would a dear friend. When you make mistakes or feel inadequate, remind yourself that it's part of being human. Instead of dwelling on your flaws, focus on growth and self-improvement. Be patient with yourself and allow space for errors, knowing that they are opportunities for learning.

Self-care is often misconstrued as indulgence—bubble baths and spa days. While these are lovely, self-care goes deeper. It's about making choices that support your mental, emotional, and physical well-being in meaningful, sustainable ways. This could mean setting boundaries with people who drain your energy, taking time off when you're overwhelmed, or saying no to commitments that don't serve you. Developing a better relationship with yourself involves recognizing that your needs matter just as much as anyone else's. By caring for yourself, you're not only nurturing your body and mind but reinforcing your self-worth.

A key aspect of your relationship with yourself is how you express your truth. Your voice, ideas, and emotions are valid, and it's crucial to create space for them in your life. Whether through engaging in creative outlets, speaking your mind, or setting healthy boundaries, self-expression is a way of honoring who you are. Writing, painting, singing, or simply voicing your opinion can be liberating acts of self-acceptance. When you express yourself authentically, you reinforce the belief that your thoughts and feelings matter. This fosters a sense of freedom and reinforces the trust you've built with yourself.

Perhaps the hardest and most important step in building a relationship with yourself is self-acceptance. We live in a world that constantly pushes us to be better, smarter, more successful. But a truly healthy relationship with yourself means acknowledging that you are enough just as you are—right now, in this moment.

Self-acceptance doesn't mean complacency; it means acknowledging that you are worthy of love, respect, and kindness even when the world is against you. It's the act of embracing your quirks, flaws, and vulnerabilities, knowing that they are part of your unique story. Self-acceptance and complacency are often confused, but they differ significantly in both mindset and outcome. Self-acceptance is about acknowledging and embracing who you are, including your strengths, weaknesses, and imperfections, without harsh judgment. It's a healthy recognition of reality, where you accept yourself as you are while remaining open to growth. Self-acceptance fosters self-awareness and encourages you to improve—not out of self-loathing but because you value yourself and want to reach your potential. For

Self-acceptance doesn't mean complacency; it means acknowledging that you are worthy of love, respect, and kindness even when the world is against you. It's the act of embracing your quirks, flaws, and vulnerabilities.

example, someone practicing self-acceptance might say, "I know I have flaws, but I'm proud of how far I've come, and I'll keep working toward my goals."

Complacency, on the other hand, is a state of stagnation or contentment with mediocrity. It often involves a lack of motivation or unwillingness to change, even when improvement is possible or necessary. One is a foundation for growth, while the other resists it.

Practicing self-acceptance is a daily effort. Some days you'll feel at peace with who you are; other days, doubt may creep in. Some days you may not be able to look in the mirror, and some days you may even hate yourself. The key is consistency—showing up for yourself every day, regardless of your mood or circumstances, and reminding yourself that you are a work in progress, and that's okay.

The relationship you build with yourself is not a one-time effort but an ongoing journey. Like any meaningful connection, it requires consistent attention and care. There will be moments of frustration, days when self-doubt shadows your mind, but those are the moments when your relationship with yourself is most important.

As you continue this journey, remember that the better you know, care for, and trust yourself, the more you'll be able to bring your whole self into all the other relationships in your life. Developing a better relationship with yourself is a gift, one that enhances your life and ripples out to positively influence those around you.

Mark my words: You are an expert on yourself. Do not get distracted by all the noise. As they say, if you stop at every dog that barks during your journey, you will never reach your destination. We all make mistakes. We all are broken. The art of fulfilled living is learning how you piece yourself together after you find yourself in pieces. By cultivating a strong, healthy relationship with yourself, you create a foundation for joy, resilience, and a life lived authentically.

Amorous Relationships

You may "find" love, but if you don't tend to it, love will degrade. True soulmates are not found; they are made and tendered. Love is not magic; it is a skill. Relationships are not static; they're an ongoing dance between two people who are constantly changing.

The beauty of a lasting connection lies in the willingness to grow both together and individually. Sometimes this means adapting to new versions of each other, allowing space for dreams to evolve, or understanding that the person you fell in love with may not stay exactly the same. A strong relationship is like a dance—you may step on each other's toes, but as long as you're willing to learn the rhythm, you'll find your way together.

I think I have a better understanding of this in my second time around. This idea celebrates the beauty of growth and change, acknowledging that healthy relationships require both individuals to evolve while still choosing each other. If our commitment to each other is not dynamic and we keep hard boundaries in how we express ourselves, we stagnate and wither away. Eventually stagnation results in disaster.

A strong relationship is like a dance–you may step on each other's toes, but as long as you're willing to learn the rhythm, you'll find your way together.

Relationships can act as both mirrors and lenses. A partner often reflects our own insecurities, strengths, and dreams. They show us who we are, even in ways we may not want to see. At the same time, they offer us a lens—a new way to view the world, new perspectives that we might never have considered on our own. In loving someone else, we find reflections of our deepest truths, and through their eyes, we glimpse worlds beyond our own. This dual role of a partner is what makes relationships transformative; they don't just connect us to each other but deepen our understanding of ourselves.

Take my wife and me, for example. I'm from Pakistan; she's from Venezuela. We come from entirely different worlds—different languages, different cultures, different religions, and different upbringing. We grew up on opposite sides of the globe, each shaped by traditions and expectations that couldn't be more distinct. She loves music and dancing, both huge parts of Venezuelan culture, where celebration is woven into the rhythm of daily life, and some of these are not part of my upbringing.

But something remarkable happens when we stop focusing on the differences and instead look at what connects us. We both share a second language, which allows us to bridge the gap between Urdu and Spanish. We've each adopted elements of American culture that give us common ground, a kind of third space where our two worlds meet. And beyond any cultural influence, we both share a deep love for family. We're both quick to laugh, both drawn to helping others, both eager to find joy in the small things.

This time around I also understood I needed to change certain aspects of myself to avoid repeating the mistakes that led to the end of my first marriage. The definition of insanity—doing the same thing repeatedly and expecting different results—resonated deeply with me. Before remarrying, I often told myself that my flaws were fixed and that I couldn't change much. I was wrong. While I might not be able to change every irritating habit, I can control how I react to things. This awareness has been crucial in my journey toward personal growth and in building healthier relationships moving forward. Relationships are complex and multifaceted. They require constant effort, self-reflection, and the willingness to change.

In so many ways, my wife complements me. She has a gift for expressing her emotions with an openness and warmth that I admire and sometimes struggle to match. She brings out parts of me I might otherwise keep hidden; together, we balance each other. What we share in common has proven to be so much stronger than what sets us apart. And in the end, the common ground we've built is far more powerful than the differences we entered our relationship with.

Relationships are about letting someone into your inner world, opening doors to places you may not even want to enter yourself. This act of vulnerability is terrifying but essential for real connection. Being able to share your fears, insecurities, and dreams is what builds trust and intimacy, creating a foundation that can withstand life's inevitable challenges.

In any deep relationship, there will be times when one person needs more support, more patience, or more understanding. Holding space for someone means allowing them to be where they are without trying to change or fix them. It's about giving someone room to process their emotions, heal, or grow without judgment or expectation. This concept of holding space reminds us that sometimes the most loving thing we can do is simply be present, allowing the other person to be seen and accepted.

Sometimes love requires letting go—whether it's letting go of control, letting go of expectations, or, in some cases, letting go of the relationship itself. Love isn't about possession; it's about allowing someone to be who they are, even if it means releasing them from your grasp. This speaks to the strength it takes to honor someone's freedom and growth, even if it means they may drift away from us.

Conflict is inevitable, but it doesn't have to be destructive. Instead, it can be an opportunity to deepen understanding and strengthen bonds. Healthy conflict means listening deeply, respecting each other's perspectives, and finding compromise without compromising respect. It's not about winning or losing but finding a path forward that honors both people. Conflict, when approached with compassion, can be a tool for growth, revealing each person's needs, boundaries, and priorities. It allows both individuals to feel seen and valued, even when they don't agree.

We must realize that beauty is found in ordinary moments, not just celebration in grand gestures. True intimacy is built in the small, everyday moments. These are the times when love feels simple: sharing a morning coffee, laughing together at a joke, doing chores side by side. In these quiet, unremarkable moments, a relationship finds its strength.

Family Relationships

Family relationships include connections between parents, children, siblings, and extended family members like grandparents, aunts, uncles, and cousins. Family relationships are often lifelong and characterized by a deep bond, mutual support, and shared history. I think the strongest bond that exists without any expectation of return is the love of parents.

I recall a story that has always reminded me of the rare and selfless love that exists in the world, especially the profound love of a mother. True, unconditional love comes with no expectation of anything in return, only a pure willingness to give. I remember the night I admitted an elderly patient, a woman in her late seventies, brought in by the police. She was frail, barely a hundred pounds, so thin and weak she seemed almost transparent. Her son—towering and muscular, a spitting image of a young Arnold Schwarzenegger—had abandoned her in the worst way.

This son, her only child, had bound her to a bed in diapers, tossing her scraps of food now and then while draining her Social Security income to fuel his lavish lifestyle. It wasn't until concerned neighbors heard strange sounds and alerted the authorities that she finally escaped his clutches and was brought to the hospital.

It was late at night when I first saw her. Her face held a look of quiet despair, a silence that seemed almost unbreakable. I leaned in and gently asked her, "When was the last time you had a decent meal?" She just looked back at me with vacant eyes, unable or perhaps unwilling to answer, as if even that simple act was beyond her.

I asked if I could get her something to eat, and she nodded. I hurried down to the cafeteria, picking up a few items, and found some grapes, thinking they'd be easy for her to eat. When I returned and placed the tray in front of her, she took one look at those grapes and began to devour them with a desperation I'll never forget—as if each one might be her last.

Afterward, as I got more details from the police officers, I gently asked if she would tell me about her son, the man who had left her in such a state. She simply shook her head, and when I pressed a bit further, suggesting she speak to the police so charges could be filed, she stopped, looked me in the eyes, and said, "He's a good boy. He'll learn from this."

Only a mother, I thought. Only a mother's love could endure such suffering and still, somehow, hold a place of forgiveness in her heart. Despite her torment, she was willing to bear every indignity, every cruelty, in the hope that her son might one day find his way. To me, that was the ultimate reflection of true love: boundless, self-sacrificing, and without expectations.

I remember reading a story a long time ago. In it, two friends were talking, and one of them said, "Did you hear? My brother just gave me a new car." His friend looked at him and said, "Wow. I wish *I* could be that kind of brother."

That response hit me like a revelation. It's a subtle but powerful shift in perspective—a paradigm shift. Most people would hear about the gift and think, *I wish* I *had a brother like that*, longing to be on the receiving end of such generosity. But the other friend's response was different. He didn't envy the gift; he admired the spirit of giving.

It got me thinking about how often we spend our lives waiting—waiting for others to be kinder, more generous, more thoughtful. Waiting for someone to be a "better" friend, sibling, parent, or partner. But what if the real power lies in flipping that expectation inward, in striving to *be* that person ourselves?

Imagine approaching every relationship with that mindset. What if, instead of hoping for a more loving partner, we focused on *being* more loving? What if, instead of wishing for a supportive friend, we *became* that friend? It's a simple shift, but it changes *everything*. Instead of waiting to receive, we find fulfillment in giving, in showing up fully and openly, in becoming the kind of person others can count on.

What if, instead of hoping for a more loving partner, we focused on being more loving? What if, instead of wishing for a supportive friend, we became that friend?

In the end, that story reminds me that the best way to make our relationships richer and more meaningful is not to wait for others to be better but to strive every day to be the best version of ourselves for them. To be the kind of brother, sister, parent, or friend that we ourselves would be grateful to have. I wish I could become like my brother and sisters.

Friendships

Friendships are born from shared interests, experiences, and backgrounds, creating bonds that can range from casual acquaintances to lifelong connections. They bring comfort, joy, and a sense of belonging, offering a safe space where you can truly be yourself. At their core, friendships thrive on trust and mutual respect, giving us the strength to weather hard times and the freedom to celebrate the good ones.

I've always believed that friends are the family we choose. Unlike the family we're born into, friendships are built intentionally. They grow through shared experiences, trust, and care. There's something powerful about investing in someone and having them invest in you in return. Often, a good friend understands you in ways others might not—they've been beside you in the moments that have shaped you and know you in a way that feels uniquely personal.

That said, good friendships don't just happen on their own. They require effort, patience, and a willingness to give as much as you hope to receive. Before you can expect loyalty or support from others, you have to be willing to offer it yourself. True friendships are built on showing up, listening, and being the kind of person you'd want in your corner.

Friendships come in all forms. Some are fleeting, tied to certain times or places in life, while others last for years, enduring time and distance. Both types matter. The short-lived ones bring joy, growth, and memories, while the long-term ones become the constants you can always rely on. Together, they remind us that life is richer and more meaningful when shared with others.

It's often said that if you can count your best friends on one hand, you're lucky. By that standard, I consider myself truly fortunate. I've had the privilege of building incredible friendships over the years, and for that, I'm endlessly grateful. Those friendships have shaped me, supported me, and reminded me that the greatest blessings in life often come in the form of the people we choose to hold close.

Relationship with God

A relationship with God is one of the most intimate and mysterious connections a person can experience, and yet it often lives in a place beyond words. It's a journey that can lead to profound comfort, boundless questions, and even moments of spiritual isolation.

I remember a story my mother used to tell me. I can still picture her on that quiet afternoon, a well-worn book open in her lap, her voice soft and steady as she shared this tale—a parable, really, about perspective and faith, about the things we often don't understand. It was a story about a woman pregnant with twins. She called them Spirit and Ego.

In this story, Spirit and Ego had been floating together in the warmth of the womb for many months, feeling only the gentle pulse of life around them. It was all they knew, and for a while, it was enough. But one day, something shifted. They felt it deep in their bones, an unsettling tug that neither could explain. Startled awake, Spirit looked over at Ego and whispered, "What is this place? Where are we? How did we get here?"

Ego, ever the pragmatist, shrugged. "This is just ... *the way it is.* This place has always been here. We've always been here. Maybe it just *happened.* A big bang or something."

Spirit smiled, thoughtful and a bit sad. "Maybe ... or maybe there's something more. Sometimes I feel like there's ... a mother out there. Something greater that created us, holding us close."

Ego smirked. "Mother? That's ridiculous. There is no one 'out there.' This place we're in, this is it. This is all there is. We're alone."

But Spirit was stubborn. "Sometimes I feel a warmth, a certain kind of love flowing in," Spirit insisted. "Maybe that's her. Maybe that's our mother's love reaching us."

"Love?" Ego rolled his eyes. "You must be going crazy. Have you ever *seen* this so-called mother? Have you ever touched her?"

Spirit fell quiet, unable to answer, though a small, persistent hope remained. Weeks passed in silence, and Spirit's questions didn't fade; if anything, they grew stronger. One day, Spirit whispered again, "I think … I think there's life after birth. I feel like there's something waiting for us. Something beyond this place."

This time, Ego couldn't contain his laughter. "Life after birth? You're losing it! How would we survive out there? This place—this womb—is the only world we know. Out there? We wouldn't even be able to breathe!"

"But what if there's something different waiting for us? What if we don't need to breathe the way we do now?" Spirit asked gently.

"Look," Ego replied, shaking his head, "you can believe whatever you want, but this is all nonsense. Just focus on what's real, what's here."

As my mother closed the book, I remember the silence that hung between us, heavy and contemplative. She looked at me with a gentle smile and said, "Sometimes, when it comes to life and faith, we're all a little like those twins. We only know the world we're in, and we might never be able to fully grasp what lies beyond it. But just because we can't see something, or touch it, doesn't mean it isn't there. Sometimes we just don't have the right lens yet, the right perspective to understand it."

It reminded me of other things, like how we know infrared light exists even though we can't see it without special tools, as it falls outside our visual spectrum.

Or how someone once told Picasso that abstract art was meaningless, and he replied, "Just because you don't speak Chinese doesn't mean the Chinese language doesn't exist." Sometimes what we call "faith" is just a willingness to believe in things we don't yet understand.

Over the years, this story has stayed with me, a reminder that there's no shame in not having all the answers. Sometimes what matters more is our willingness to keep asking questions, to remain open to possibility. I've noticed how people in their final days, some the staunchest nonbelievers, often find themselves drawn to something beyond themselves—grasping for a sense of peace, a glimmer of meaning. Perhaps it's not about who's right or wrong; perhaps it's about finding something to hold on to, something that brings comfort in the end.

Of course, there's another side to this, the part that nags at us when we see suffering in the world—the senseless violence, the cruelty, the things we can't explain. It's tempting, in those moments, to reject any notion of a higher purpose, to question why the innocent suffer and the wicked sometimes go unpunished. But if there's one thing I've learned, it's that faith—whatever form it takes—should never be used as a weapon. The worst thing we can do is make someone feel foolish or small for what they believe, whether they worship the sun or await a second coming.

> There's no shame in not having all the answers. Sometimes what matters more is our willingness to keep asking questions, to remain open to possibility.

In the end, perhaps it's all about perspective. Like those twins in the womb, we're all just trying to make sense of the world we're in, searching for answers we might not be ready to find. And maybe, just maybe, the most profound act of faith is to accept that some mysteries are bigger than us and that it's okay not to understand it all.

But perhaps one of the greatest paradoxes of faith is that both certainty and doubt often coexist in the same heart. Some days you feel connected to something vast and loving, like an invisible embrace that holds you even when everything else falls apart. Other days, you feel a hollow ache, an emptiness where you expected to find peace. The silence can be deafening, and you wonder if it's all just an illusion.

And yet, even in the doubt, there's a certain kind of seeking that can feel holy. The act of reaching out, questioning, and even wrestling with God becomes a form of devotion in itself. People who question the nature of God, or even God's existence, are often the ones who care most deeply. Their doubt isn't the absence of faith—it's a sign that they're wrestling with the mystery in a way that's profoundly honest.

Spiritual connection with God, then, isn't always about unwavering belief. Sometimes it's about holding on, even when your grip feels tenuous. It's about walking through periods of darkness, trusting that light will come again, or at least hoping it might. It's about finding sacredness in the questions as much as in the answers.

In the end, whether someone believes or doesn't believe, feels connected or is distant, the spiritual journey is deeply personal. It's not something that can be easily defined, proven, or dismissed, and, most importantly, not something that can be forced. Our spiritual journeys start in a dialogue—sometimes quiet, sometimes loud—that lives within the heart. And perhaps that's what makes it so powerful. The relationship with God, with belief and unbelief, with certainty and mystery, is a dance that's as old as humanity itself.

Gentle Goodbyes; Failing Forward

All relationships may eventually come to an end—whether through time, distance, or circumstance. The one relationship that endures, regardless of the nature of your beliefs, is the relationship you have with yourself. However, what truly defines you as a person is how you manage yourself when a relationship is coming to an end—whether you handle it with grace, self-respect, and empathy or allow it to fragment the core of who you are.

There's a certain restraint one needs to show when saying goodbyes, to ending things with grace and intention. As much as we'd like to believe that the good things in our lives will last forever—relationships, careers, friendships, even entire empires—the truth is, most things have a natural shelf life if left unattended. Everything we hold dear will eventually change and inevitably come to an end, even if that ending does not arrive until death.

When a chapter closes, whether it's letting go of an employee, ending a relationship, or stepping away from a place you once called home, the way we handle those goodbyes says a great deal about who we are. It's easy to be defined by how we enter things—our enthusiasm, our charm, our promises. But how we exit often speaks more deeply to our character. Are we leaving with bitterness and resentment or with a sense of peace and respect?

A graceful farewell, even when it's painful or complicated, can leave behind a lasting impression. It shows that we honor the time that was shared, the lessons that were learned, and the growth that came from the experience—even if it didn't end the way we might have hoped. Saying goodbye with kindness and respect not only honors the past but also shapes the future, setting the tone for the relationships and opportunities that are yet to come.

Ultimately, it's not just about closing a door; it's about leaving it open enough that those on the other side feel respected, understood, and valued. Gentle goodbyes are not a sign of weakness; they're a mark of wisdom. They remind us that in every ending, there's a chance to create something new—a space for healing, growth, and maybe even forgiveness. It's in these moments that we define not only who we've been but also who we're becoming. There is an exact parallel in recognizing this aspect of a gentle goodbye to the way that failure can allow us to grow. Just as we shift our view of what an "ending" can mean, we can begin to see an opportunity for new success rising from the failure of falling down. It's another way that we can "fall forward." We come to see the arc of our own evolution.

Dealing with disappointment, frustration, and even betrayal is never easy, no more so than experiencing failure. These emotions can feel overwhelming, raw, and completely justified. When we've been hurt or let down (or we have hurt or let ourselves down), it's only natural to feel anger, sadness, or bitterness rise up. We have every right to feel the way we do. But how we choose to navigate these emotions can make all the difference—not only for our own peace of mind but for everyone involved.

It's tempting, in moments of pain, to lash out or to retreat, to let anger dictate our actions or to wall ourselves off entirely. But when we react impulsively to hurt, we often end up creating even more pain for ourselves and others. Instead, finding a way to process these emotions thoughtfully—whether that means talking to someone we trust, giving ourselves space to cool down, or taking time to reflect—can lead us toward a more grounded response.

Choosing to respond with intention doesn't mean we're ignoring our feelings or pretending everything is okay. Rather, it's about acknowledging our emotions without letting them control us. It's about deciding, consciously, what kind of person we want to be, even when we've been wronged. In those difficult moments, the way we choose to respond says more about us than the actions of those who have hurt us.

Handling disappointment and betrayal with grace isn't about excusing the behavior or suppressing our feelings; it's about protecting our own peace. It's about allowing ourselves to feel hurt but not letting that hurt define our actions or our character. By finding a way to process these feelings with compassion and dignity, we're not only giving ourselves a path to healing but also setting a powerful example of strength and resilience for everyone around us.

Relationships are the foundation of our lives, shaping who we are and how we grow. These connections can take many forms—whether with colleagues, friends, family, or partners—and each comes with its own challenges. The key to holding our relationships together lies in mutual respect, open communication, and a willingness to nurture the bond. It's about truly seeing the other person—acknowledging their needs, emotions, and flaws—while also being honest about your own. Empathy, patience, and forgiveness serve as the glue that binds relationships, especially during difficult times. But above all, a healthy relationship requires balance: giving without losing yourself and receiving without taking for granted. Ultimately, the strength of any relationship is not measured just by how long it lasts but by the effort, care, and love that go into keeping it whole.

AFTERWORD

Resilience is silent and deep, like roots. It doesn't announce itself. It doesn't explode outward. It doesn't fall. It doesn't break. It simply always is. And you are.
—VICTORIA ERICKSON

And with that, if you are still with me, you found my message in a bottle. Make sure yours is spoken and heard. I hope that you have discovered ideas that resonate within you and that you give yourself permission to be open to new ideas, new perspectives, and new relationships. If you do, you will have developed the graceful art, the fearlessness, to fail forward.

ABOUT THE AUTHOR

Irfan Ali, MD, is a highly accomplished physician and the president, CEO, and cofounder of several leading healthcare organizations. He earned his medical degree from the University of Karachi in Pakistan and completed his residency in internal medicine at the University of Massachusetts. He also received a fellowship from Beth Israel Deaconess Medical Center at Harvard Medical School.

From his humble beginnings as a carpet cleaner to his success as an entrepreneur and the president of a large healthcare group, Dr. Ali has combined his medical expertise with a deep passion for social causes. He is the founder of Pioneer Medical Group and Pioneer Medical Foundation, which provides free medical services to thousands of homeless, refugee, and indigent citizens. The foundation also conducts multiple projects in Florida to support the underserved.

Dr. Ali's career is distinguished by his creativity and dedication to emotionally intelligent patient care. Art and literature enhance Dr. Ali's approach to medicine: he often draws parallels between the complexities of medical practice and artistic expression, and he enriches his own life with interests like painting, writing, and photography.

Beyond his medical practice, Dr. Ali is an international keynote speaker known for improving leadership skills and communication and developing strategies. He lives in Tampa with his wife and their five children—four beautiful daughters and one son.